Don't Stop THE MUSIC

To Beth

Don't Stop THE MUSIC

DANA KEY
with
STEVE RABEY

Zondervan Publishing House
Grand Rapids, Michigan

Don't Stop the Music
Copyright 1989 by ForeFront Communications Group

Published by the Zondervan Publishing House
1415 Lake Drive, S.E., Grand Rapids, Michigan 49506

Library of Congress Cataloging-in-Publication Data:

Key, Dana.
Don't stop the music / by Dana Key with Steve Rabey.

"Youth books."
ISBN 0-310-51681-1
1. Christian rock music—History and criticism. I. Rabey, Steve.
2. Title.
ML3187.5.K5 1989   89-5781
261.5'7—dc20   CIP
                                                              MN

All Scripture quotations, unless otherwise noted, are taken from the *Holy Bible: New
International Version* (North American Edition). Copyright © 1973, 1978, 1984 by the
International Bible Society. Used by permission of Zondervan Bible Publishers.

Edited by David Lambert
Interior Designed by The Church Art Works
Printed in the United States of America

To my whole family:

Thank you so much for your love, patience and encouragement. Especially you, Dad, who taught me by word and deed to obey the calling of God rather than popular opinion.

Dana Key Personal Management:
Brock & Associates
Nashville, Tennessee
Dana Key Correspondence:
P.O. Box 24947
Nashville, Tennessee 37202

Contents

Foreword

Every kid has dreams. Little did Dana and I realize when we met in the first grade that the Lord had put us together to fulfill a very specific dream. Music was always the focus of our dreams, and in the years that followed we almost let that dream destroy us. We found out that music was an incredibly powerful tool -- and we used it for all the wrong reasons. We chased stardom, but never found it. We strove for acceptance, but never achieved it.

Dana making music at home with daughter, Scottie, and son, Andrew.

In our senior year of high school, we found out what our dream was really all about. Within a two-day period, both of us made a decision that would follow us the rest of our days: We gave our lives, our hearts, and yes, our dreams to Jesus Christ.

Music took on a different dimension for us. Not only did we praise God through our music, but we began to write songs that simply communicated to others the hope that we had found in Jesus. Style was not important; in fact I'm not sure it was ever discussed. But we soon found out that there would be years of discussion to follow; every well-meaning Christian had a different opinion of music and Scripture verses to back it up.

So then--has my friend Dana just written another book to be filed with the rest of the opinions? I don't think so! First of all, Dana draws from a well of experience that few authors share. He has actually seen with his own eyes the power music possesses, both good and bad. Secondly, he has the biblical foundation and education necessary for forming a truly Christ-centered opinion.

Together, Dana Key and I were told that if we continued to play Christian rock music we would rot the brains of every church-going young person in America. Instead we've seen thousands upon thousands of young people turn their lives over to Christ. Many of those fans have become leaders in the church and are winning others to Jesus.

Everyone has dreams. That is our dream. That is why Dana wrote this book. He gives real answers to the difficult questions surrounding music. May you use these answers to better serve the Lord.

God bless you,

Eddie DeGarmo

Introduction

It was after midnight in Kansas City.

The concert had ended. The auditorium was emptying out. And the road crew was busy packing up our instruments and all the sound and lighting equipment.

Eddie DeGarmo and I had finished talking and praying with young people in the counseling room. For us, that's a big part of every evening; even though it's emotionally draining, we take it seriously.

Now, after a long evening, Eddie and I were making our way to the bus and our next concert, more than 300 miles away.

We felt pretty good about the evening's concert. We had played well, which always pleases us. And we were especially happy about the invitation I had offered to young people to accept Christ. Nearly two dozen teenagers had made first-time decisions for Christ.

Nearly everyone had left the parking lot, except for one young lady who had been waiting for us since the concert ended. She didn't look happy to see us. Instead she looked angry. As she headed toward us, she yelled out: "You describe your music as rock and roll. Did you know that the expression 'rock and roll' is a metaphor for sexual intercourse?"

After the initial shock wore off, Eddie responded. "Who told you that?" he asked.

"My pastor," replied the young woman.

Then Eddie asked, "Did the words 'rock and roll' have anything to do with sex in your mind before your pastor told you that was what they meant?"

She hesitated for a moment. "No, I guess not," she answered quietly.

Fanning the Flames

It's been more than a decade since Eddie and I started playing our brand of Christian rock music. That's more than ten years of making records, playing concerts, writing songs, preaching to and praying with young people, and traveling for thousands of miles.

During those years we've heard our share of criticism and arguments. Some of it has been at close range, like that woman who stopped Eddie and I on our way to the bus. Some of it has been less personal, like the time an evangelist went on TV criticizing everything Eddie and I—and a lot of other Christian musicians—stand for.

The hardest times for us were our first years, in the late 1970s. Critics like Bob Larson and others were drawing loud cheers from Christian audiences for saying that there was no such thing as Christian rock.

"Talking about Christian rock is like talking about Christian striptease dancers," they would say. People would cheer.

"It's like talking about Christian abortionists!" they shouted. People cheered again.

"Rock music is from hell! It's Satan's music. There's nothing we can do to improve it. We should best leave it alone before it drags us to hell, too!" More cheers.

During the early 1980s the argument seemed to cool down. At least Eddie and I felt like we were getting less criticism from people than we had during the band's earliest years.

But in the mid-80s, the flames of controversy were fanned again, and the anti-rock argument heated up.

Who knows why controversies come and go. Maybe it was the increasingly blatant sexuality of artists like Prince and George Michael, the violence that seemed to follow some rap artists, and heavy metal rock's growing popularity that made more people more angry about more and more of popular rock music.

In the Christian music scene, perhaps groups like Stryper made some people question what was going on with Christian rock. And maybe people were upset by the "crossover" Top 40 success of Amy Grant, a talented artist Eddie and I accompanied for her two live albums.

I don't know why the arguments heated up in the past few years, but one thing was certain in my mind: That evening in Kansas City I prayerfully vowed to stand up and speak out in defense of Christian rock and the ministry I felt God had called me to.

Why I'm Speaking Up

As the bus pulled out of Kansas City and began the long ride north to Minneapolis, I sat up and thought about the woman who had approached us with her pastor's condemnation of rock and roll. I thought of the verbal attacks that had been made on us and other dear Christian brothers and sisters.

I sat up most of that night—watching the lights go by outside the bus and thinking about how much pain the controversy over music was causing, and of the need for a book like this.

Before that night I had never pictured myself as a defender of contemporary Christian music. Sure, I believed God was using it. And Eddie and I could see firsthand that He was using our ministry. In fact, the letters we receive in our office every week attest to the fact that somehow God uses our concerts to lead people to Christ, and even to lead some to consider lives of Christian service.

But should I be the one to write the book defending it? I certainly didn't feel that I was a scholarly pop culture apologist, but at least I had done my homework:

- I've been making Christian music for a decade, and I've been keeping my eyes and ears open to people and God the whole time;
- I've been reading most of the Christian books on rock that have been published during the past 15 years or so; I studied cross-cultural ministry during

my theology studies at Bible college, and even wrote one of my college papers on the use of popular music as a cross-cultural evangelism tool;

- I worked for Youth for Christ for four years, serving as Memphis Area Director for 20 YFC clubs and participating in the evangelism and discipleship of thousands of young people;

- and I'm a servant of Christ who believes that God can guide and use the words of my mouth, the meditations of my heart, and even the humble jottings from my pen!

Believe me, I wish I didn't have to write this book. I wish the current controversy didn't exist. And I don't intend to make arguing and debating with Christian brothers and sisters a habit. I would much rather do more pleasant work. But I've gotta do what I've gotta do!

The Consequences of the Controversy

The biggest reason I'm writing is that I believe you and I are at a critical place in time right now. God is starting a revival among young people today, and I believe he is using music as part of this revival. I don't want to see it hindered by arguments and division.

Young people are terribly important to God's work. As Billy Graham has said, 85% of all conversions to Christ happen to people who are under 18 years of age. God grabs many people in their youth, and it's a good thing, too.

But because today's young people face so many ob-stacles, a pessimism seems to pervade their world. This pessimism has many aspects, but it includes doubts about their own personal lives, the difficulties they feel they'll find when they enter the job world, the fear of nuclear annihila-tion, the fear that there won't be any clean air to breathe or water to drink when they're older, and so many other problems.

Problems with sex, for instance. Sex has come out of the closet since I was young. Sex has always been a temptation for young people, but TV and movies leave a lot less to young people's imaginations than when I was a teenager. And today sex can kill you.

I've seen God use Christian music as a tool to touch and melt young people's hearts. When combined with a clear presentation of the gospel message, music is a powerful weapon in the battle for kids' souls. I don't want the current controversy to stop the music—thereby hindering God's work.

Let me share a letter a young girl wrote to Eddie and me:

Dear DeGarmo & Key:

I'm a very concerned Christian. I really enjoy your music, but lately I've run into some controversy about Christian rock. It seems like everybody is fighting over whether it is right or wrong.

Personally, I'm more concerned about the life of the performer. Do their lives match up to what they are singing?

That's why I am writing. I would like to know your convictions and feelings about different issues that come up in your walk with Christ.

For a while I have been listening to secular rock, mostly Madonna, Chicago, Huey Lewis, even a little bit of Bon Jovi and Motley Crue. The Lord showed me how wrong that was, but now I'm finding that many Christian rockers listen to the same thing, and Amy Grant even sings with them.

I'm really concerned. Are Christians starting to be like the world in ways they shouldn't be? How do you think Christians should be separated? Also, what are your goals for your ministry? What are your concerts like? What church do you attend?

The answers to these questions would really help me. I know Christian performers and ministers are in a tough position and I pray for you a lot.

In Christ, Carol P. in Pennsylvania

What's in this Book for You (And Carol)

For Carol and thousands more, I hope this book will answer some of your questions and give you a clearer understanding of what God really desires for each of us, and how music might be used to help some of us move in that direction.

This book is for you, no matter who you are:

- *a young person struggling to find an answer about what kind of music you should be listening to;*

- *a parent trying to understand why your kids' music sounds so strange to you;*

- *a pastor or youth leader seeking some solid principles on which to base your recommendations to people who look to you for guidance;*

- *or maybe a strong critic of Christian rock who is reading this book to look for more anti-rock ammunition.*

Whoever you are, I pray that God will use this book in your life. I wish I had had a book like this ten years ago.

May God challenge you to catch the vision for what he's doing with young people today. May he fill your mind with wisdom and insight. May he challenge you to new levels of participation in the work of his body today. And may he strengthen you as you read.

God bless you.

PART

1

DON'T STOP THE MUSIC

CHAPTER

1

WELCOME TO
THE FAMILY

The big bell rang out, signaling to the hundred or so students hanging around outside Hillcrest High School in the snow and ice that it was time to head for class.

Zombie-like figures shuffled through the door, still whispering about highlights from the past weekend. As I headed in out of the snow and the cold, Eddie DeGarmo, my friend since first grade and my partner in numerous rock bands, tapped me on the shoulder.

"Hey, Dana," he said. "There's something I want to tell you."

It had been a bad weekend, and I was feeling kind of depressed. I certainly didn't feel like being at school. "OK," I said, "but make it quick or we'll both be late to chorus class."

"Dana," Ed said, "Yesterday I went to church."

The idea of Eddie going to church surprised me. Maybe he saw the shock in my face, because he forced the next words out of his mouth as if he wanted to get the whole thing over with.

"Dana, I gave my life to Christ."

God has different ways of getting our attention. For me, as a high school senior, God seemed to be working overtime to wake me up.

I had just broken up with my girlfriend, and was feeling pretty lonely. I had just lost an idol—Jimi Hendrix, who had died of a drug overdose. And the week before, I had gone to a concert by the rock band Mountain and heard a guy I had never heard of before named Mylon LeFevre talk about how glad he was that Jesus had come into his life.

So when Eddie came up to me and told me about accepting Christ, I felt like I had just been hit by a ton of bricks. I wasn't too excited about the idea of discussing Jesus in the school hallway, so when the second bell rang (signaling that we were late for class), I suggested that—at the risk of suspension—we duck into a nearby storage closet to discuss things further.

I moved around a box or two, made myself comfort-able, and prepared myself to hear the whole story of how

Eddie had given his life to Christ.

As Ed spoke, I reflected back on a similar experience that had happened to me when I was twelve years old. It was then that my father, a dedicated Christian, first explained to me my need to trust Christ as my Savior. Even though it had been many years before, I could still remember the yearning feeling my father's words created in my heart.

That same feeling was returning with every word that Ed spoke. Before I knew it I was down on my knees in the closet committing my life to Jesus.

I'm not sure who truly led me to the Lord—Eddie or my father. But I do know that after that closet prayer meeting, my life began to change radically.

No Sunday-Go-to-Meetin' Clothes

There was one radical change in my life right off—I decided that I should start going to church.

Finding a church was no small task, even though there was a church on pretty nearly every corner in Memphis. The problem was finding a church where Eddie and I would fit in.

At the time Eddie and I looked pretty wild. Our limited wardrobes were firmly rooted in the 60's hippie culture. My hair was long. The only pants I had were blue jeans, and most of them had holes in them. I didn't own a single shirt with a collar on it. I didn't have any Sunday-go-to-meetin' clothes.

What Eddie and I wanted was a church that would help us grow closer to Christ while letting us keep our hair and jeans. And to our surprise, it didn't take us long to find one. Eddie and I quickly became two of the most unusual-looking Southern Baptists anyone had ever seen.

Sure, we seemed strange to some of the Christians in our church, but they accepted us all right. At the same time, this new Christian world we now found ourselves in seemed very strange to me. The language ("Praise God!"), customs (going to church three times a week), and dress (lots of shirts, ties and polyester) of my newfound Christian brothers and sisters seemed pretty foreign. But I adjusted quickly, because I really wanted to grow as a Christian. I knew I needed to be around Christians, even if they did seem a little odd.

What's That Sound?

Eddie and I were happy in our new lives and new church. We were reading our Bibles, praying, witnessing to others about our faith, and growing by leaps and bounds. Overall, my life was filled with joy and contentment—except for one thing: music.

Music had always been a big part of our lives. Eddie was the first to play in a band—playing organ in a band called the Chants with his brother Larry.

After the Chants broke up Eddie and I started a band called the Sound Corporation. We were a five-piece band that played songs like "Sittin' on the Dock of the Bay" and "Land of a Thousand Dances," and songs by groups like the

Dana hamming it up with Steve Taylor, rhythm guitar player in Dayton, Ohio

Young Rascals and the Beatles. We played at a bunch of little parties throughout junior high.

When we got to ninth grade we started a new band called Globe. This was a ten-piece outfit with horns and a rhythm section. Before long Globe was playing two or three nights a week. Eddie and I were making pretty good money for high-school kids. When we were seniors, Globe got a record deal with London Records.

All of this stopped when we gave our lives to the Lord. We suddenly felt uncomfortable about playing some of the songs Globe played. And pretty soon we found ourselves out of a band.

Our church, like many others in the South, didn't have much use for secular rock and roll. To most church folks, rock music meant Elvis, Jerry Lee Lewis, and other sexually suggestive performers who had fallen away from the Lord. And now that I'd become a Christian, I agreed wholeheartedly with their criticism of rock and roll's negative moral values. With the encouragement of several older brothers in Christ, I threw away all of my rock records. Gone were all my records by Jimi Hendrix, Grand Funk and Deep Purple. Gone was the music of my generation.

What made matters worse for me was that there wasn't anything I could replace my old music with. We had never heard of Christian rock—and, in those days, neither had anyone else. So we tried to appreciate Southern Gospel music. Ed even went so far as to join a gospel group from the church. But when I listened to Southern Gospel music on the radio I could only stand it for three or four minutes at a shot.

Eddie and I felt like we were lost in a time warp. We were desperate for Christian music that we could enjoy, but there wasn't any to be found.

Making Music Again

It became clear to Eddie and me that if we were going to have any Christian music we liked, we would have to make it ourselves. Out of sheer desperation, we began to write and play rock-and-roll songs with Christian lyrics.

Our plan was to keep our writing and rehearsal sessions a secret. But word got out; people began showing up.

At first it was just a friend or two of mine or Eddie's. But each week more people showed up at our sessions. Pretty soon there were a hundred people coming to listen to us write and rehearse Christian rock and roll.

We were pleasantly surprised and encouraged by the turnout. It showed us that we weren't the only people in the world who were untouched by traditional gospel music. We realized, in fact, that an entire generation felt a void in their lives that popular gospel music didn't fill.

Our rehearsals were turning into little concerts and evangelism sessions. It was a wonderful and exciting time. Christians were bringing unsaved friends to band practice and they were getting saved by the dozens. Eddie will say an "Amen" to this because one of the people who came to know the Lord at our rehearsals was a young woman named Susan. Now Susan is Eddie's wife.

As secret rehearsals exploded into a mini-subculture revival, we became more aware of two things: first, that people were hungry for positive, Christian rock music, and second, that this same music, when surrendered to God's hands through prayer and the Holy Spirit, could be used by God as a powerful evangelism tool.

With our newfound optimism, we decided that it was time to take our music out of the closet and put it on the streets. This is where we encountered our first real obstacle.

Band on the Run

There's a feeling shared by many Christian musicians, and that feeling has been expressed in songs by Larry Norman, Mark Heard and others. It goes something like this: I'm too religious for the secular folks, but I sound too secular for the Christians.

That's exactly the situation Eddie and I found ourselves

in as soon as we tried to take our music out of the rehearsal hall and out to the world. In all our previous bands, we had been accustomed to playing in nightclubs. But now, no self-respecting nightclub would have us. We were simply too Christian for them.

We desperately wanted to play somewhere, so we borrowed some flatbed truck trailers and began playing and preaching on street corners and in parking lots. It didn't take many nights of dodging beer bottles and insults before we became discouraged with our new street ministry. Many nights we longed to be back in our cozy and safe rehearsal studio. But what we longed for even more was for others to hear our music. So we decided to take our music to our family—the church! We felt certain they would see the value of our Christian rock, but we'd been Southern Baptists long enough to know better than to use the word "rock" in describing our group to pastors. After all, we didn't want too many red flags going up right up front.

So when we told a pastor we knew about our band, we described ourselves as a gospel group. I mean, we were a gospel group, kind of, weren't we?

It worked. The pastor invited us to play at his church. We anxiously awaited the chance to share our music with our family.

The trucks rolled up to the church doors the next afternoon. As we carried our amps into the church, I could read the concern on the pastor's face. I hurriedly walked over to him and reassured him that we were a *gospel* group. (I don't remember if I had my fingers crossed.)

We began our debut church appearance by cranking up a song in our normal, high-decibel fashion. But no sooner had we begun than I saw some of the church's elders stand up in the back of the auditorium. Believe me, they weren't standing to praise God for our music. Their angry red faces were proof of that.

Next, they headed toward the podium at a very brisk pace. Quickly, I leaned over to Ed.

"What do you think they want?" I asked.

His response was immediate: "I think they want to lay

hands on us."

And I don't think I have to tell you that this laying on of hands was not the same kind of positive, brotherly experience that Paul described in the book of Acts!

Thus began my initiation into the seldom boring, always energetic, and usually divisive debate over the place of rock music in the church and the Christian life.

What's your position on the great debate? Are you a young person who likes your music with a noticeable beat? Are you a pastor or teacher who is concerned with the effects music has on kids? Are you a parent who is concerned about what your children hear? Or are you a "musical agnostic," someone who is unsure about music and what the whole issue is all about?

Whoever you are, and wherever you find yourself on the issue right now, I want you to know this: I've been there myself.

I've wrestled with the place of music in my own life. I've struggled over what kinds of music are helpful or harmful for young people who are under my ministry. And I'm a parent who is deeply concerned about the type of music my own children absorb and digest.

Perhaps you've already guessed what my position is in this grand debate. I'm a follower of Jesus who wholeheartedly believes that God has called me to make music that is both contemporary and Christian.

And I believe that God can use rock in at least two ways: to help Christians love and praise him, and to introduce nonbelievers to him in a new and meaningful way.

As you read the rest of this book, I hope you will come to understand how I've arrived at my position. And I hope I can help you cut through some of the noise and get to the heart of the issue.

CHAPTER

2

DIVISION IN
THE FAMILY

I should have seen what Eddie and I were walking into. I thought it was going to be a warm, friendly meeting with some leaders of our church—just like they said. But it was much more than that.

We were ushered into a small Sunday school room. The pastor was the last one to enter; he closed the door behind him. Then one of the men began a prayer: "Oh Lord, we ask you to give wisdom to all here today. And we ask you to help Ed and Dana, and to help them see what's on our hearts today. Thank you for helping us to see things your way. Amen."

The echoes of the prayer were hardly dead before the interrogation began.

"Dana, do you and Eddie really want to be used by God?" asked the pastor, allowing only a millisecond's pause before adding, "Well, then here's what you have to do."

The prescription that followed was a familiar one, and it involved all kinds of external codes and laws: we should cut our hair, we should wear nicer and more respectable clothes, and we should tone down our music.

There was some disagreement among the men at the meeting. Some thought we were doing good things, and they appreciated all the young people who had begun showing up at church after hearing our band.

But others weren't so happy. "The elders are complaining about the way you boys look," said one.

The meeting ended with our agreeing to change our appearance. But our hearts were heavy.

Sound Wars

People who have grown up in the last three decades have grown used to something that earlier generations never knew, as least not as we know it: the power of music to divide one generation from another.

I didn't realize how bad the problem was until I was sitting at a music seminar with Bill Gaither and I heard Bill say, "Music used to be the universal language, but it's not anymore."

Bill went on to point out that many of the top-rated television shows of the 50's were centered around popular music, such as the prime-time show called "Sing Along With Mitch." Other popular shows like Ed Sullivan and Jackie Gleason's variety shows included music for the entire family.

But in the '80s that kind of show is an impossibility. Music, once a unifying power in society, is now one of the most divisive issues around.

It used to be that a man was known by the company he kept. Now he can be sized up by the music he listens to. Dad likes his country and western, Mom prefers her classical, while older brother bangs his head to heavy metal and little sister likes new wave.

The battle lines are drawn, and the sound wars rage from room to room, often with each family member criticizing the other's taste in music. Dad tells his son, "That junk all sounds the same to me. How can you tell one song from the next?" Mom smugly thinks, "Anything but Bach and Beethoven is crass and commercial."

Music Anywhere/Anytime You Want It

Not only are musical styles growing and diversifying, but with some of the technological developments of the 20th century, music to suit your narrowly defined personal taste is always available—whether you're driving, bathing, jogging or flying in a jet plane.

In previous centuries music was only available when musicians made it for you on the spot—either at church, in the opera house, or perhaps during an impromptu concert from a musically gifted family member. Today music is in your face (or at least in your ears) anytime and anyplace. America has more radios than people. American families own an average of six radios, and 81% of American families own stereo systems. (Dan & Steve Peters, *What about Christian Rock?* Minneapolis: Bethany, 1986, p. 15.) The average adult listens to three hours of music a day; a young person listens to up to six hours of music daily.

The net result of this onslaught of easily accessible music is that people in the 20th century are developing very personalized musical tastes. As the printing press revolutionized the way people read in the 15th century, so technology has revolutionized the way people consume music in our own century.

A Power to Divide or Unite

As music of every imaginable variety (and even some unimaginable varieties) becomes increasingly available, we can plainly see music's ability to both unite and separate. The band U2 can get 18,000 fans swaying and singing "Pride (In the Name of Love)," while others passing by the noisy arena hear only cacaphonous noise.

Why is music so controversial? Because music is more than just music. It communicates a number of messages about lifestyles as well. Music has evolved into a sophisticated form of communication for groups and subcultures.

The metal heads like their music loud and heavy and their clothes dark and studded. The punk subculture has its own look, vocabulary and background music—including the Dead Kennedys and the Violent Femmes.

To adults, who themselves have their own subculture, all the youth subcultures look a little strange. The music just completes the strange package of appearances, vocabulary, dress, behavior, and even values and beliefs.

Dan and Steve Peters, two Christian youthworkers who have written extensively on rock music, talked about the effect of music and subculture in their book, *Why Knock Rock?* "As a language . . . music has the capability to communicate only to the culture which produces it. It often confuses outsiders even as people with different languages sometimes fall prey to misunderstandings and frustrations due to communications failure. This occurs with music of different generations."

Division in the Family

Dividing the Human Family
and the Church Family

In Genesis, God confused the language of the people of earth at the Tower of Babel. Music is having a similar effect today, as unfamiliar sounds in music lead to distrust, fear and prejudice.

Unfortunately, this confusion and division is affecting the church, too. The church family is just like the human family we described earlier, except this time around Dad likes southern gospel music, mom likes the classic hymns, brother likes Stryper and sis likes Russ Taff.

To make matters worse, we each tend to believe God prefers *our* particular style of Christian music because, after all, isn't that the particular style God uses to bless and touch us?

In a recent issue of *Contemporary Christian Music*

DeGarmo & Key performing live in Zaire, Africa.

Magazine, Harold Best, Dean of the Wheaton College Conservatory of Music, tackled the problem: "Why do Episcopalians approve a certain kind of music that the Pentecostals don't? And why do the Lutherans in Germany approve a certain kind of music that the Lutherans in Chile won't? Churches approve music they're most used to."

It's a subject I've explored myself, as I've explored the way Christians across America worship God and express their faith in a variety of ways.

Unity in the Midst of Diversity

Something that has taught me a big lesson in having patience and tolerance for the different ways people appreciate music and other things has come through my travels with the DeGarmo & Key band. We've traveled thousands of miles over the past ten years—including a trip to Africa with the people from Mission Aviation Fellowship—and I've had my eyes opened to the many ways people express their faith in God.

I was raised a Southern Baptist, and naturally assumed Christians all over the world worshiped God as the people in my church did. I can still remember how amazed and shocked I was the first time I was in a church where people spoke in tongues. It freaked me out!

Now I'm more used to being in an Assemblies of God church one night, a Presbyterian church the following night, and a Catholic pentecostal church the night after that. Over the years I've realized a lot of Christians are different from me. And you know what? That's OK!

Christians like different kinds of music. Take the band's bus driver, Gary Jines. He loves country music, and in between his talking on the bus CB radio he listens to Hank Williams and other country artists. Hank Williams isn't my cup of tea, but as we're riding on the bus and I see Gary listening to his country music I try to enjoy it with him, and I try to learn what he likes about the music.

And as I'm listening with him I ask God to help all of us not go to war over the once-universal language of music.

Our Prayer for Unity

Back in 1987 Eddie and I were taking heat for our music. A well-known television evangelist was criticizing our band's ministry on his show.

We were hurt. We were frustrated. And frankly, we wanted to lash out at this man. We wanted to argue with him. Our thoughts were not always Christlike.

But we prayed about the attacks on us and other Christian musicians, and what came from those prayers was a song called "Brother Against Brother (It's Not Right)." I would like to end this chapter with that song:

Will you say a prayer for me
I'll say a prayer for you
We've got a long way yet to go
Will you take a stand with me
I'll take a stand with you
We can help each other grow
It takes a little bit of understanding

I'm not just like you
Cause a brother don't judge a brother
Can't we agree that's true, cause
You know it's not right
Brother against brother

(By Eddie DeGarmo and Dana Key. © copyright 1987 by DKB Music/ ASCAP, a division of the ForeFront Communications Group, Inc.)

While in Pittsburg, DeGarmo & Key received a commerative collage for their release of D & K. Pictured are Dusty Rhodes, WPIT Radio, Pittsburg; Mike Gay, The Benson Co.; Greg Morrow; Tommy Cathey; Dana Key; Ron Griffin, ForeFront Comm.; Eddie DeGarmo; Dan Brock; and Steve Taylor.

ROCK AND ROLL
OUT OF CONTROL

We don't know exactly why it happened, but the mayor of Cincinnati decided there was going to be a "DeGarmo & Key Day," and we were to receive a proclamation from him just before our 8:00 concert.

But before we even got to the auditorium, Ed and I were invited to appear on a local radio talk show. I assumed that they wanted to ask us about the music and ministry of DeGarmo & Key.

We arrived at the station, were greeted warmly, given cups of coffee and hustled into the studio. It was then that the talk show host told us what was coming. "We're doing a show on the efforts by the Parents Music Resource Center for a nationwide music labeling system," he said.

I gulped. Being on the road and in the middle of a tour, we hadn't had lots of time to follow the news. But I knew that Tipper Gore, the wife of Senator Albert Gore from my home state of Tennessee, had formed the PMRC and was asking the music industry to voluntarily label their records in order to warn parents of potentially offensive language.

I remember seeing a TV news clip from earlier that week. The women of PMRC, whom Frank Zappa had sarcastically called "the Washington Wives," had appeared before a Congressional Committee pleading their case.

"And, by the way," our host calmly added, "you'll be debating Frank Zappa."

Suddenly I was doing more than merely gulping. Zappa was an exceptional musician and a very intelligent man. Not long before I had seen Zappa making logical mincemeat out of PMRC representatives on Ted Koppel's "Nightline" show. I had also seen portions of his testimony before the Congressional panel. Needless to say, I was not excited about debating him.

I wondered whether this was how St. Paul felt when defending the faith in front of skeptical opponents, and I prayed silently that the Lord would give me wisdom so that I wouldn't embarrass Him.

By God's grace, we were able to see the fatal flaw in Zappa's logic. Zappa and others opposing the PMRC called

*what the group was trying to do "censorship." The PMRC,
they argued, was trying to prohibit the making and distribution of certain records. In reality, all the PMRC was doing
was seeking a labeling system that would inform concerned
parents.*

*Eddie and I thanked God for his help and left the studio
to receive our plaque from the Mayor and play that
evening's concert.*

*But I continued to prayerfully consider the issues
surrounding secular rock music.*

Over the years Eddie and I have listened to a fair share
of secular rock music. Surprisingly, we never paid a lot of
attention to the words—as musicians, we concentrated
instead on the music, the arrangements and the production
of the albums.

Then one day I went into a Christian bookstore and
picked up two books. One was *Why Knock Rock?* by the
Peters Brothers, and the other was *Raising PG Kids in an X-
Rated Society* by the PMRC's Tipper Gore. These books
opened my eyes to some of the lies being spread through
rock music—lies about love, about God, about parents,
about everything!

As I talked to other people—Christian musicians,
young people, pastors, youthworkers and parents—I discovered that they too were unaware of the propaganda in the
lyrics of popular rock songs.

Believing that Satan works best in our ignorance, I
decided to include this chapter on secular rock music. I
wanted people to be aware of rock's darker side. And,
maybe, when we see how evil some rock music is, we can
quit fighting over Christian rock and focus on the bad stuff.

Rock's Big Lies

As I began listening more carefully to the lyrics of
secular rock, I began to see a pattern. I saw that some of the
songs were taking good subjects—like love—and perverting

them. As a result, these songs were spreading lies about God and the world he created for us to enjoy.

The more I heard, the angrier I became. I started keeping notes on some of the worst songs. And I've provided the lyrics to some of these songs in this chapter.

My hope is that you will see how some rock music perverts God's truth, and that you will learn to guard your mind and heart from these lies.

Lie 1: Love = Sex

For generations, one of the most popular topics in music has been love. But in the last twenty years or so, there have been a lot fewer songs about love and a lot more songs about lust. Is it so surprising that, today, many people think love and sex are the same thing?

One of the biggest sex hits of recent years is "Sugar Walls" by Sheena Easton:

> *"You can't fight passion*
> *When passion's hot temperatures rise*
> *Inside my sugar walls."*

The song is erotic and explicit. But it says nothing about love—all it describes is the physical changes a woman's body goes through. Sure, it's provocative, but what does it teach us about love?

And how about Tone Lōc's "Wild Thing":

> *"Couldn't get her off my jock, she was like static cling,*
> *But that's what happens when bodies start slappin'*
> *From doing the wild thing."*

In other songs you can find any kind of sex you want. If it's "Let's treat women as sex objects" that turns you on, you can go to Ted Nugent's "Wango Tango," or a hundred other songs and music videos.

How about gay sex? Then tune into Frankie Goes To Hollywood's hit song, "Relax."

Incest? Check out Prince's song, "Sister":

*"My sisters never made love
To anyone else but me...
Incest is everything it's said to be."*

If that's not enough, how about sex with a dead person, which is described in Slayer's song, "Necrophiliac."

Don't get me wrong. I'm not against sex, and God isn't either. After all, he made it, and he obviously designed it to be enjoyed. (Don't take my word for it, check out the Bible. Read some of God's erotic poetry in the Old Testament book, "Song of Solomon.")

But God's truth is that sex is part of a committed love which is expressed in marriage. These songs and many more pervert this truth and equate sex with love. Please don't let these songs fool you.

Lie 2: Love = Sex + Violence

Not only do many songs confuse sex with love, but many also add sexual violence to the mixture, glorifying rape and murder.

Multi-platinum Guns 'n' Roses, in their song "Anything Goes," tries to make sexual violence sound like fun:

*"Panties 'round your knees with your a-- in debris
Doin dat grind with a push and a squeeze
Tied up, tied down, up against the wall
Be my rubbermade baby and we can do it all
My way your way anything goes tonight."*

Here's Motley Crue's "Live Wire":

*"I'll either break her face
Or take down her legs
Get my ways at will
Go for the throat*

Never let loose
Going in for the kill."

There are many other songs that combine sex with violence, including the Judas Priest song, "Eat Me Alive." And the videos shown on MTV are frequently criticized for their depictions of violent sex. But I don't need to include hundreds of examples here. It's clear that violence is not what God intended between lovers.

Lie 3: Even Without Sex, Violence Is Good

Many songwriters sing about pure violence in glowing terms. I don't know what makes singers think that killing, maiming and mutilation are fun topics, but they seem to be popular with a few artists, such as the Dead Kennedys, who wrote the song "I Kill Children":

"I kill children
I love to see them die
I kill children
I make their mothers cry."

Slayer (what a positive name for a band, right?) mixed violence with some anti-Christian feelings in their song, "Kill Again":

"Kill the preacher's only son
Watch the infant die bodily dismemberment
Drink the purest blood."

It's unlikely that songs like these will make normal, healthy young people run out and commit violent acts. But not all young people are healthy and normal—many are hurting and confused, lost, afraid, lonely. And these young people may be susceptible to these lies about violence—as well as those about suicide.

Rock and Roll Out of Control

Lie 4: Suicide Is Good

Thousands of teenagers kill themselves every year. Suicide rates for teens rise every year. So why would anyone write songs that seem to encourage kids to take their own lives? Unfortunately, many artists are doing just that.

Suicide has been a popular topic in rock music ever since Blue Oyster Cult's popular hit, "Don't Fear the Reaper." Since then, songs like Black Sabbath's "Killing Yourself to Live," AC/DC's "Shoot to Thrill," Pink Floyd's "Goodbye Cruel World," and Ozzy Osbourne's "Suicide Solution" have appeared.

Some of these songs have even been discussed in court trials; the parents of young people who have taken their own lives have argued that the songs influenced their children's decisions to take their lives.

Can songs about suicide actually convince young people to attempt suicide? I don't know. But how can any responsible artist record anything that might even accidentally induce a young person to take his life?

Eddie and I know that suicide is a serious issue for many young people, and many kids at our concerts tell us that they are very uncertain about life. It was for kids like these that Eddie and I wrote the song, "Teenage Suicide":

> "I don't want to hurt nobody
> It's just that I know I've had enough
> There's too much pain and hatred
> I think I'd rather be dead
> Than to live without mercy, hope or love."

We go on to sing about the hope we find through Jesus. And we also provide phone numbers for crisis counselling centers that help kids deal with the feelings that lead to suicide.

If you're sad and depressed about life, don't listen to the lies saying that suicide is good. Turn to God and some good people you can trust for help!

Lie 5: It's All Show Biz

Some of rock music's fake philosophies aren't found in the lyrics— they're found in the lifestyles of the artists who make the music. Artists love to brag about their orgies, parties and bad habits.

And is it all true? Sometimes not. For some artists, the evil, rebellious lifestyle is only part of a carefully designed image. Many of these artists privately lead a normal life. But sometimes it is true; for some artists, the evil you see on stage is a genuine part of their evil lives.

Only God knows the truth about people's private lives. It's impossible for us to judge whether Ozzy Osbourne is really into Satanism, as many have argued. But whether the performer truly embraces sin as his philosophy of life does not really matter. What matters is that millions of naive teenagers are convinced that their rock idols live out sin-filled lifestyles on and off stage and are tempted to imitate them.

Imitating much of the evil that appears on stage at some concerts would be difficult; in some cases, it could get you thrown into jail. Take, for example, this description of concerts by the Beastie Boys, found in *Teen Vision Magazine:* "Their on-stage displays have included spraying beer at the audience, simulated masturbation, obscene comments and gestures between songs, mouthing the exposed breasts of a bikini-clad caged dancer, encouragements for girls in the audience to expose their breasts, and an inflatable phallic symbol reportedly 20 feet in length."

Hit Parader magazine reported that Iron Maiden's singer Bruce Dickinson was slapped with a lawsuit for allegedly undressing a woman on stage against her will during an Iron Maiden concert in Buffalo, New York.

In the interests of fairness, I'll add that many rock artists have done some very positive things in public. Jon Bon Jovi and others have spoken out against drug abuse. Bruce Springsteen, Peter Gabriel, Sting and others have worked with Amnesty International. And others have united to raise consciousness and funds for the hungry and dying in Ethiopia and elsewhere. But it is my fear that the good some rock artists do is greatly outweighed by the damage others cause in young people's lives.

Lie 6: Drugs and Alcohol Are Good

Drugs have been endorsed in rock music since I listened to rock in the 60s and 70s. And somehow the fact that Jimi Hendrix, Jim Morrison of the Doors, and Janis Joplin—three of the earliest and biggest rock artists—died with the help of drugs didn't diminish the popularity of drugs in music.

During the last few years alcohol—not pot or cocaine—has become the drug of choice among many rockers. So now, when teenage alcohol abuse is on the rise, many in the secular rock world are making things worse.

David Lee Roth proudly tells *Hit Parader* magazine, "The Jack Daniels I drink on stage is real." Nikki Sixx of Motley Crue tells the same magazine, "My bottle of Jack Daniels is my best friend in the world. It's always there to give me support, even when my friends aren't."

Songs like Journey's "Lay It Down" add fuel to the fire:

"Whiskey, wine and women,
They get me through the night
...what I'm really needin'
Ah, double shot tonight."

And Lita Ford's "Kiss Me Deadly":

"Had a few beers, gettin' high
Sittin' watchin' the time go by
Uh huh, it ain't no big thing."

As usual, rock is full of ironies. Michelob beer provides money to artists like Eric Clapton in exchange for promotion at the artists' concerts. Even Pete Townshend, a recovering alcoholic, accepted beer dollars for the financing of a tour by his band, the Who.

It's true that rock music alone won't make a young person run out and become an alcoholic. But still, the lyrics of some rock songs and the life styles of some rock musicians encourage kids to abuse drugs and alcohol—as well as their own bodies.

Lie 7: God Doesn't Matter

One extremely popular—and dangerous—lie found in many rock songs (as well as many television shows, movies, and books) is that God doesn't matter.

Creative songwriters have found a million or more ways to express the fact that God is dead, or asleep, or missing in action, or irrelevant, or out of the picture of our lives in some other way.

Van Halen expressed it in their hit, "Best of Both Worlds":

"You don't have to die and go to heaven
Or hang around to be born again
Just tune into what this place has got to offer
Cause we may never be here again."

Van Halen picks up the same theme in "Mine All Mine," which describes the frustrations the writer has encountered in his search for truth:

"Yeah, the search goes on...
Staring at the sun
Searching for the light
Almost ended up blinded."

The writer has given up on organized religion because of the charlatans that preach the gospel. But even when he looks at Jesus he gets confused:

"You got Allah in the East
You got Jesus in the West

Rock and Roll Out of Control

Christ, what's a man to do?"

In the end, the singer concludes, "Stop lookin' out, start lookin' in." In other words, God isn't out there—or at least you can't find him. So give up. Look inside yourself and find truth there.

Of course, another lie is that Satan is God—an idea found on many records. But you're not dumb. You know how to tell black from white.

Just remember—God *does* matter, regardless of what you hear on rock albums or television.

Lies 8 through 5,000

We can't cover all the lies in rock music in this chapter—that would take a very big book. But here's what you can do to fight rock's lies: First, focus on God's Word and the truth that's in it. Second, keep your ears and eyes open to what the music around you is saying. And finally, stay away from music that is trying to tell you lies.

Dana with his wife, Anita

We're Fighting a Battle!

If you're a parent or youthworker, chances are you're pretty upset about some of the propaganda being spread through rock music. I'm upset, too. And I've got some suggestions for things we can do together to fight the evil in rock. Maybe, working together, we can make the world of rock music a safer place for young people's ears.

First, *don't overreact!* When I was a teenager I was shown a film in high school which said that smoking marijuana would drive a person crazy, cause him to become a thief, and cause birth defects. I was no expert, but I knew these claims were exaggerated. So I didn't take any part of this film on drug abuse seriously.

In the same way, hysterical, uninformed claims about rock music will cause valid criticism to be disregarded. Don't say, "All rock music is evil," when it would be closer to the truth to say, "Some rock music is evil." Don't say, "Rock music causes suicide," when you should say, "Rock music may have been an influence in some suicides."

By going overboard with your criticisms, you may cause the good things you're saying to be ignored.

Second, *get smart.* You must be informed. To combat the negative influence of much of rock music, you need accurate information.

I doubt that anyone has expressed that need better than Dee Snider, vocalist for the band Twisted Sister. This is what Snider said at the PMRC Hearings before Congress in the Fall of 1985: "As a parent myself and as a rock fan, I know that when I see an album with a severed goat's head in the middle of a pentagram between a woman's legs, that is not the kind of album I want my son to be listening to."

But how many parents would even know if there are pentagrams and goats' heads on their children's album covers? How often do they go to concerts with their kids to see what is going on on stage and in the audience?

We need to be informed. Start with your kids' records, tapes, posters, T-shirts, and other paraphernalia. I've listed

Rock and Roll Out of Control

a number of other sources of good information about the current rock scene at the end of the chapter.

Third: *get together.* Groups have more influence than individuals, so organize your friends and neighbors to write letters and make phone calls about offensive rock concerts or clubs in your area. If you're a member of an existing group, such as the P.T.A., Kiwanis Club or even a Sunday school class, bring the issue before your group. Call or write your city officials, asking them not to rent publicly owned facilities to offensive groups. Ask your city council to follow the example of the San Antonio, Texas, city council, which passed a law restricting unaccompanied minors from attending lewd and violent rock concerts. Call or write record store owners and ask them not to sell records with pornographic lyrics. If the 7-11 convenience stores can be successfully pressured to take pornographic magazines off their shelves (and they were), record stores can also be influenced.

And don't forget to call or write your representatives in Washington. Ask them to introduce legislation that will force the record industry to keep their promises to let parents know what is being said in song lyrics.

Fourth: *focus on the real enemy.* I find it difficult to understand why some preachers have chosen to attack Christian rock rather than taking aim at godless secular rock. Why have Tipper Gore and the PMRC, a secular organization, become leaders in exposing the dangers of secular music while many in the church continue to bicker over Christian rock or backward masking?

Debating the merits of Christian rock while letting the destructive power of secular rock continue unopposed is like two doctors arguing over the proper medicine while the patient silently dies. Our energies need to be unified and directed at the real enemy: that segment of the rock world that is clearly evil and dangerous.

Fifth: *fight lawlessness with law.* After the PMRC hearings in 1985, the recording industry promised to begin voluntary labeling of offensive lyrics. But these promises have not been honored. Now it's time for legislation.

Many get uncomfortable when I talk about legislation.

"What about the First Amendment?" they ask. "What about freedom of speech?" But the laws and Constitution of this country were never intended to protect pornography, and many concerned parents would agree with singer Smokey Robinson that much popular music is "auditory pornography."

Currently, laws restrict access to pornographic magazines and R-rated movies. Why, then, can any young child go into a store and buy a record praising having sex with a corpse, or attend a concert where there is simulated sex on stage?

Godless rock groups do have first-amendment rights to freedom of speech. But we can restrict the age of those who are exposed to them. Let's try to see that promoters require the audience attending these R-rated concerts to be at least 18 years old.

Sixth: *just say no!* Get involved with your kids' choice of music. When they bring an objectionable album home from the record store, don't burn it—instead, discuss it with your kids, and then take it back. Don't forget that the underlying motivation in the secular record industry is money; if you return an album to the store, your action hurts them where it counts—in the pocketbook. Even if the store refuses to refund your money, you've made a lasting impression on the store manager's mind.

The same principle applies to concerts. When your child asks permission to go to an unacceptable concert, get tough for his or her sake. When necessary, say absolutely not. When enough kids stop laying out $20 bills for concert tickets, the obscenity will stop. And don't forget that giving your child well-defined boundaries will give him or her emotional security for a lifetime.

Seventh and finally: *provide an alternative.* To expect your child to give up Motley Crue for Lawrence Welk is unrealistic and unnecessary. Provide a more attractive alternative: good, meaty Christian rock.

Today there are a multitude of talented Christian musicians producing state-of-the-art records that are both spiritually challenging and uplifting. In sharp contrast to the limited distribution of these records ten years ago, they're now readily available in record stores and bookstores worldwide. Artists such as Petra, Amy Grant, Morgan Cryar, Mylon LeFevre, Servant, Stryper and others are providing us with quality alternatives to secular rock. God forbid that we allow ignorance or apathy to prevent us from taking full advantage of these alternatives!

Portions of the secular rock scene are dark and evil. One light for young people at the end of this dark tunnel is the light of Christ presented in the music and lifestyles of dedicated and talented Christian musicians. As the evil world of secular rock continues to darken, Christian rock will shine that much more brightly.

D & K with manager Dan Brock and a few of the courageous missionaries and pilots sharing God's love with these Zairian children in Zaire.

CHRISTIAN ROCK AS AN ALTERNATIVE

Buddy is a good friend of mine and an ordained South-ern Baptist minister. Over the past ten years, Buddy and I have had a number of debates about Christian rock music. Maybe debate is too neutral a word. We've had heated arguments! But we've always remained friends. And some-how our disagreement hasn't kept us from keeping in touch with each other over the years.

It had been a while since I had heard from Buddy, then out of the blue I got a call from him. "Uh, you'll never believe this, Dana," he said, fumbling for words. "I just wanted to tell you that I've become one of DeGarmo & Key's biggest fans. I just went out and bought all of your albums for my son, Joshua."

What prompted Buddy's sudden change of heart?

"Well, Josh came home from one of his Cub Scout meetings the other day, and he was singing a song. I asked him to sing it for me, and he began singing 'We're Not Gonna Take It,' by that rock band Twisted Sister. It made me realize that I can't shelter Josh from rock music. Sure, I can keep it out of our home—but I can't guard Josh while he's at school, or even when he's at a Cub Scout meeting.

"Dana, I just called to let you know that I realize I was wrong before. Now I understand what you're doing—and I appreciate it. Thanks."

What do young people like today? It doesn't take a lot of brains or energy to figure that out. Just look at page 68 of Allan Bloom's bestselling book, *The Closing of the Ameri-can Mind:* "Today a very large proportion of young people between the ages of ten and twenty live for music. It is their passion; nothing else excites them as music does; they cannot take seriously anything alien to music."

The fact that kids love music is something Eddie and I realized years before I read Bloom's book. And taking that love for music as an assumption, we've been making Chris-tian music for kids for a decade.

But when we started DeGarmo & Key, there weren't many Christian record labels fighting to sign and record new bands. Those were tough times.

Christian Rock as an Alternative

Waiting for a Miracle

Eddie and I sat around in quiet despair, waiting for a door to open that would allow us to pursue the Christian music ministry we believed was God's will. This was after three years of searching and questioning, of laying down our musical instruments and desires and saying we would never play again.

Finally, with our parents' encouragement, we decided to take the next step—going into the studio to record a demo tape. But our first obstacle was money. Eddie and I were poor college students. My worldly possessions included a $150 Volkswagen van, an electric guitar, an amp and several pairs of well-worn blue jeans. So we prayed—and, just as those who prayed all night for the Apostle Peter's release from prison found it hard to believe when Peter appeared at their doorway, we were equally hesitant to believe that God had answered our prayers when the door finally opened.

To my surprise, Chan Prosser, my boss at Youth For Christ, loaned Eddie and me $300 to purchase one day of studio time. Chan was sad to see me leave YFC, but supported my vision for the band.

With our $300 in hand, we headed for a local studio. Our session began early and lasted late into the night. By the time we finished we had four or five songs on tape that we were proud of.

The next step was to send the tapes to Christian record companies, and wait.

And wait.

And wait.

Then the responses began to flood back to us—all rejecting our tape and our music. It was discouraging and confusing.

Then, out of the blue, Pat Boone telephoned Eddie. As Eddie says, "When the guy on the phone said, 'Hi. This is Pat Boone,' I thought he was kidding!" Soon we realized that this was no joke, and that Pat had a deep and genuine concern for the spiritual health of young people. Pat feared that many American young people were being irreparably damaged by rock music, and he challenged Eddie and I to become part of the cure.

Away from the Fringe

Soon Eddie and I were recording our first album. Ten albums and ten years later we're still making music to reach kids with the gospel and to counteract the destructive influences of much of secular rock.

Much has changed over the past decade, but one thing really sticks in my mind. That's the change in the arguments against rock music.

Ten years ago it seemed like only a small (but very loud!) portion of the lunatic fringe of Christianity opposed rock music. Today, more and saner voices are objecting to rock's negative influences. The criticism of rock has moved away from the fringe.

Among those voices is Dr. Allan Bloom, the renowned social scientist from the University of Chicago and author of

ana in concert

Christian Rock as an Alternative

The Closing of the American Mind. As Bloom writes: "The lyrics celebrate puppy love as well as polymorphous attractions, and fortify them against traditional ridicule and shame...The words implicitly and explicitly describe bodily acts that satisfy sexual desire and treat them as its only natural and routine culmination for children who do not yet have the slightest imagination of love, marriage or family" (p. 74). Bloom says that a steady diet of contemporary rock is one of a number of factors causing today's young people to become morally weak and flabby.

Building a Christian Consensus

A decade ago, Christian books about rock were full of silly arguments about how rock music is bad for house plants and the body's internal organs, about how rock's beat came straight from hell or from African blacks (which, according to some of those authors, was the same thing), or that anything that sounded like rock was bad, regardless of what the lyrics were saying.

But in that decade, God raised up a number of authors who spoke eloquently about the evils of rock while offering Christian rock as a sound alternative. There's still plenty of uninformed mud-slinging going on in Christian circles, but, thank God, there's also some saner, sounder writing going on by people like Dan and Steve Peters, Al Menconi, and Bob Larson.

The Peters brothers, two pastors from Minnesota, have taken plenty of heat for their opinions—not only the heat of being on national TV shows like "Nightline," but also the heat from album bonfires! It's true that the Peters brothers are unapologetically critical of much of the evil in secular rock—they're also quick to point out the alternatives. They not only warn the church of rock music's real and present dangers, but they also offer Christian rock as a wholesome alternative.

But they haven't done so without criticism. They printed this letter in their book, "What about Christian Rock?":

Dear Peters Brothers,

I was at your seminar when you began to play ex-
amples of what you called "Christian" contemporary music
as an alternative to secular rock music. Well, I grabbed my
children and headed for the door, because the small portion I
heard looked and sounded just like the ungodly music you
had just been knocking!

I don't understand! One minute you are condemning
rock and roll and the next you are offering young people the
same perversion, the same demonic beat and rebellious
sound under a different label. You are Christians and say
you are concerned for the well-being of our children. Don't
you realize that music is a "wolf in sheep's clothing" and
could never be pleasing to God?

But the Peters Brothers are convinced that there is a
life-and-death difference between secular and Christian rock
in four major areas: lyrics, lifestyles, goals and graphics.
And they continue to recommend Christian rock.

Al Menconi is a former school teacher who saw firsthand the impact music can have on kids' lives. For the past
few years, Al has been traveling the country offering his
rock music seminars in churches, schools and auditoriums.

But Al is just as strongly in support of Christian rock as
he is against much secular rock. In fact, he says listening to
Christian music is one practical way to do two things the
Bible commands us to do: "pray without ceasing" and
"write God's law on our hearts." Al says good Christian
music can help us meditate on God and his will for us.

Bob Larson was one of the earliest Christian speakers
and writers to discuss the evils of rock music. Beginning in
the 1960s, Larson wrote books critical of rock's roots, message, philosophy and impact. For many years, Larson was
equally critical of Christian rock. But in the 1980s, he
changed his tune. Larson still speaks out against godless
rock, but now he recommends Christian rock as a healthy
alternative.

Christian Rock as an Alternative

Fighting Our Battles Together

War does strange things to people, and one of those strange things is that it sometimes creates unlikely allies. The U.S. joined forces with the Soviet Union in order to stop Hitler in World War II. Today feminists and fundamentalists have joined together to fight pornography.

Likewise, many concerned parents and pastors who prefer Lawrence Welk and George Beverly Shea to DeGarmo & Key have united with our band to wage war against a common musical enemy that is poisoning the minds of millions of teenagers.

Personally, I don't care what kind of music you like. Maybe you don't even like music. That's fine with me. But we're in a battle for the minds and souls of today's young people, and if more Christian people pray for ministries like DeGarmo & Key, Petra, Amy Grant, Stryper and others, more kids can be freed from Satan's lies.

Jesus calls Christians the "salt of the earth." In Christ's day, salt was used as a preservative; today, Christians must be a moral and spiritual preservative in our world. Our very presence on this planet prevents the world from becoming thoroughly rotten and decayed. And without the presence of Christians, the world would plunge headlong into decadence.

God calls His people to follow Christ's command to be "in the world" but not "of it." Eddie and I—and many other artists—are using contemporary music as a vehicle to let our light shine to a darkened world.

Some would prefer we adopt a "monastery mentality": "If I build walls high enough or travel far enough away from this decadent world, I can obtain a higher degree of purity." But only Christ can make us pure from sin. No amount of running from the world can save us.

The answer isn't higher walls or more distance. The only answer is more salt! We need more Christians with the courage to let their light penetrate into dark places. We need to rub shoulders with those who are taking the spiritual war to the enemy.

We need more Christians to act as moral and spiritual preservatives in our homes, on the college campuses, at the work place, and in every other setting—all of us invading the world with the light of Christ.

Eddie and I aren't called to be Christ's witnesses on the factory floor or in an office or at school, as many of you are; we're called to let our lights shine from a stage. But *where* a person serves the Lord isn't important—it's the servant's heart that counts.

And the desire of our hearts is to serve as a preserving agent in the world of entertainment. It is with that goal that our musical ministry continues. Please pray with us that our salt will remain strong and that our light will not burn out.

Going Further

For more information about the books and materials offered by the people mentioned in this chapter, please contact:

The Peters Brothers
Truth About Rock
Box 9222
North Saint Paul, MN 55109

Menconi Ministries
PO Box 969
Cardiff by the Sea, CA 92007

Bob Larson
PO Box 36480
Denver, CO 80236

CULTURE AND THE
GENERATION GAP

It was a cold winter day in Louisville, Kentucky. We were in the middle of a tour and I had been struggling with a cold for several days. Now it seemed to be getting worse.

The guys in the band gathered around me for prayer. We prayed and prayed that I would be made well, but the laryngitis remained. Concert time was just six hours away.

And, besides the concert, there was another reason I wanted to feel better and get out of bed. That afternoon in Louisville, there was to be a great basketball game between two longtime southern rivals: the Louisville Cardinals and the Memphis State Tigers, the team from my own hometown.

But my cold grew much worse, so instead of going with the rest of the band to the basketball game, I was taken to a nearby emergency room. I missed it all—the basketball game of the year as well as a DeGarmo & Key concert.

I felt terrible, both physically and emotionally, so Eddie came to my room that evening to console me. But he seemed troubled by something himself. "Dana," he said, "today I saw Louisville Cardinal fans with red paint on their faces and some even had red streaks in their hair. On the stadium floor were the Memphis State Tiger fans with blue paint on their faces and hair."

I knew he was getting at something, but I wasn't sure what it was. "So what's the point?" I asked.

"Dana, why is it all right for kids and adults alike to wear paint on their faces and streaks in their hair at basketball games? Why is it OK for these basketball fans to act crazy, angry, emotional, and everything while screaming until the rafters shake? Why is that kind of behavior considered normal at a sporting event—but weird or even demonic if it happened at a rock concert?"

Dogs Don't Dance

What is culture, anyway? Anthropologists and social scientists say culture is one of the things that makes people different from animals, plants and rocks. The trappings of culture are all around us: our clothing, our cars, our houses. And then there are all the things normally referred to as cultural: art, movies, literature and music, for instance.

Culture is uniquely human, and it's a reflection of the fact that we're created in God's image. Culture shows that we, like God, are creative and personal.

It's the fact that culture is for people and not animals that makes cartoons like "The Far Side" and "Garfield" and the Snoopy character in "Peanuts" so popular. It's just funny to see animals acting as if they were a part of human culture.

Sure, dogs will wear sweaters—if their owners make them. But most dogs would prefer to wear the fur they're given. Dogs don't buy carpet for their dog houses. Dogs don't dig Def Leppard. And dogs don't dance. The ability to enjoy culture gives us the opportunity to appreciate all kinds of creative things that people produce—everything from Mozart to Metallica. But when people disagree about what is good and bad in our culture, the result is often anger and bitterness.

This chapter is about the arguments that erupt over culture, and what we can do to make things better.

Double Standards Aren't Better Than One

Tensions between cultures are unavoidable. Glenn Kaiser of Rez Band put it like this: "The past is often the key to the future; each generation comes into its own culturally—its own dress, language, vernacular, music styles, etc. There will always be an old guard who dislikes, rejects and fights against new fashions and trends."

Sometimes this tension is called a generation gap, because it seems that every generation looks back with a tear to the so-called good ol' days, when music was pure—and so were teenagers.

Sometimes the people who look back longingly to the good ol' days get their eyes out of focus and begin to see things that don't really exist. They ignore sins of past generations and magnify the sins of today's young people.

Others have a different type of eyesight problem. Their focus is not on the past—their focus is on everyone but themselves. They see the sins of the rest of the world, but not their own. They see the dust-mote in their brother's eye, but not the log in their own.

Both of these problems of eyesight—the looking back to an imagined perfect past, and the looking away from one's own sins—lead to the troubling problem of double standards. And if you look carefully, you can see the ghosts of double standards popping up in a lot of the arguments against contemporary Christian music and the people who make it.

A Catalog of Double Standards

As I've read and heard some of the critics of Christian rock over the past decade, I've compiled a list of double standards that show up in their criticisms. Here's a look at some of the most common double standards.

"Rock Is the Cause of the Sins of the World."

To hear some people talk, you would think there was no sin before rock music arrived on the scene in the 1950s.

These critics lay the blame for an entire listing of social sins and ills, including homosexuality, drug abuse, teenage pregnancies, abortion, violent crime, and other problems, right at the feet of the generation that gave birth to rock and roll. For them, all of our social problems began with Elvis Presley and the Beatles.

These critics describe pre-rock popular music as if it were free from sexual or corrupting content. Unfortunately, they seem to have forgotten the lyrics from some of their favorite songs, such as "I'm in the mood for love simply because you're near me." They've forgotten the swooning girls at Frank Sinatra concerts. They've forgotten that "Lovers' Lane" was a creation of their own generation, which was the first one to have cars to kiss in.

Don't get me wrong—I'm not defending rock's current excesses, and I'm not suggesting that things are the same today as they were in the 50s. Things are much worse. Teen pregnancies are on the rise. Drugs and sex now kill. And song lyrics are much more blatant. But pregnancy, drug abuse and other sins are an inheritance from earlier sinners—not a new invention.

Dana with Eddie on stage.

Show Biz Blues

DeGarmo & Key have received their share of criticism, but few have taken as much heat as the Christian band Petra. One nationally televised anti-rock crusader criticizes Petra for carrying tons of valuable equipment on tour.

One thing that critic forgot to mention is that his very criticism of Christian rockers was made possible by tons of equipment—his valuable television production and distribution equipment.

Is equipment wrong? Or does the answer to that

question depend on how the equipment is used? Is it OK to spend millions on TV equipment to reach a television audience but wrong to spend thousands on sound and lighting equipment to reach a concert audience?

Only in It for the Money

One critic says that Christian rockers use their music as a money-making gimmick. And it's true that there are one or two Christian artists who are capable of selling a million records or packing concert halls across the country. One or two.

The truth of the matter is that most Christian artists make great financial sacrifices to remain true to their calling in gospel music. Add that truth to the fact that, according to Ted Koppel of "Nightline," the critic who made these accusations goes home every night to a house that is worth $1.4 million, and the criticisms about money begin to sound hollow.

Dressed for Success

One critic condemns Christian musicians for their clothes and hairstyles. According to this evangelist, Christian artists are keeping in step with fashion trends started in the world of secular entertainment.

I like the response the guys in Stryper make when they are criticized for their outfits. "Who dresses like the world?" they ask. "It's the people in the three-piece business suits who dress like the world!"

I'm sure Stryper's spandex outfits and zany stage antics aren't everyone's cup of tea, but they aren't the only ones to dress like the world. We all do it, in one way or another. And those Christian leaders who dress in silk suits, Rolex watches and huge gold rings aren't necessarily following in the footsteps of the humble Galilean who had no place to lay his head.

Conversion? What Conversion?

Do people really come to know Christ at Christian rock concerts? One critic flatly says that no one ever has. I hate to break that news to you if you're one of the thousands of people who have come forward to make a decision for Christ at a DeGarmo & Key concert.

What makes me angry about this criticism is not that he's criticizing us—we probably deserve to be criticized. It's that he's deciding where God can or can't work. That's putting God in a box, and my experience with the Lord tells me we shouldn't do that.

Following Up

Another criticism says that any conversions that may accidentally happen at a concert aren't properly followed up, and that these young converts die on the vine for lack of good Christian fellowship.

I can't speak for all Christian artists, but I know that many do solicit the help of local believers in an effort to funnel new converts into local Bible-believing churches. Many groups, including DeGarmo and Key, have frequently (at our own expense) visited cities well in advance of our performances to help prepare the supporting churches. And we've often invited youth pastors and pastors from a wide cross section of denominations to attend meetings to plan counseling and follow up of the converts anticipated in their city.

My observation, based on my years of experience, is that when someone is converted at a Christian rock concert, they get more attention than they would if they came to know the Lord through watching TV. Who is there to follow up with the converts of TV evangelism?

One Standard for All

Former Eagles drummer and vocalist Don Henley once said that there are three sides to every story—yours, mine and the cold hard truth. He wasn't singing about the controversy over Christian rock music, but he certainly could have been.

In this chapter, we've looked briefly at some of the most common double standards used in criticizing contemporary Christian music. My responses to these criticisms aren't intended to be exhaustive or airtight; I'm just hoping to demonstrate that much of the criticism is inaccurate and unfair.

Meanwhile, as the arguing goes on, souls are dying for the lack of knowledge of Christ. And many Christian young people are staying away from the encouragement and inspiration that can be found in Christian music. They're also troubled by the double standards they hear in much of the criticism of rock music by their elders. Teenagers today are observant, questioning, and hungry for answers that ring true.

Jesus told his disciples that the Pharisees struggled to take splinters from the eyes of some, while they themselves were blinded by a log. The anti-rock crusaders may have some valid criticism of contemporary Christian music—but they will never be taken seriously by young people until they remove the obvious double standards from their own lives and ministries.

TOOL OF SATAN OR TOOL OF GOD?

My phone number used to be listed in the Memphis phone book. That was before the arrival of "the Crazed Caller."

I didn't know his name, his age, or where he lived—but I did know four things about him: he seemed somewhat mentally unbalanced; he was a big fan of DeGarmo & Key; he thought I could help him; and he would do anything he could to talk to me on the phone.

On a typical day, he would call three or four times. I don't know when he slept, but he seemed to think I never did, because he would call me at all hours of the day and night.

I cared about this mysterious caller, and I prayed for him often. But he began calling me so often that I had to come up with a solution. I told all my friends, "Look, this guy is driving me crazy. If you want to call me on the phone, let my phone ring once, hang up, and call me back."

That helped—but one big problem remained. Some nights when my family was sound asleep, he would call three or four times and let the phone ring over and over.

So I tried unplugging the phone—but that meant I couldn't receive calls from people I needed to talk to.

Finally, I broke down and got an unlisted phone number. And my problem with the Crazed Caller was over.

But you know what? Never during all of these problems did I think that the problem was really with the phone itself. I knew the problem was with the Crazed Caller, who was abusing and misusing the phone.

Tools Can Be Used for Many Purposes

One of the biggest questions people have about rock music is whether God can really use it for his purposes. It's an important issue, and one Eddie and I hear raised often.

The Bible tells us much about what is right and what is wrong. There are right and wrong actions (praying for and caring for people are right, but murder, lying, and theft are wrong). There are right and wrong attitudes (love and compassion are right, but anger, envy, and lust are wrong.)

But do you know what? There are few *things* — meaning concrete, physical objects—that God says are wrong.

Look around you at all the objects we have in our world. Most of them can be used for good *or* bad purposes. Their "goodness" or "badness" isn't part of their inherent nature; it depends on how they are used by humans—whether for good or for bad.

That's why I told you about my mysterious caller. By itself, my phone was just an inert, passive object. My friends used the phone to talk to me and tell me things I wanted to hear. But in the hands of the mysterious caller, the phone became a major cause of discomfort and distress (as well as many sleepless nights)!

You can apply this principle of good and bad uses to almost any object. Look at guns. Misused, they can kill innocent people; used properly, they can defend your family or country from thieves or invaders.

Or look at automobiles. In the hands of a drunk driver, a car is a deadly weapon. But on the other hand, an ambulance is a vehicle that brings healing and mercy.

Music is like automobiles. It's a vehicle that can be used to bring good things or bad. It can lead you closer to God, or it can lead you further away. It's a tool that can be used for many purposes.

Music and Lyrics

Some people say, "The beat and tone of rock music sound like they are straight out of hell." Many take this criticism one step further, saying that the music—and all who make it—are demon-inspired, or demon-possessed.

And it's true that some of the music of secular bands like Skinny Puppy can sound hellish. It's strange to my ears, and I don't like to hear it. But that's OK. I don't have to listen to it. Meanwhile, others will think country music or Tiffany sound bad.

(But *sound* is not the important issue. It's meaning. It's what the song is saying—and the *lyrics* of a song are what gives us that meaning. We talked about lyrics in chapter 4, so I won't go into that here. But since the sound of rock music causes so much concern, I want to discuss it further.)

I believe that music (particularly instrumental music) is absolutely void of moral qualities for either good or evil. This is not to say that there is not good instrumental music or bad instrumental music. Instrumental music can be good or bad, but that isn't a theological issue—it's an artistic one.

The "goodness" or "badness" of instrumental music is based on the performers' competence and skill. If the music is played without skill, it is bad. If it is performed skillfully, it is good. Therefore, a particular piece of music could be considered bad, yet not immoral. And some music could be considered good, yet immoral.

Aren't you glad I've cleared this up for you?

Dana fine tuning his guitar before a concert.

Tool of Satan or Tool of God?

Music Is Used in Many Ways

Today, popular music is being used for bad purposes. But it has been that way for a long time. And Christians have developed some pretty creative ways of dealing with the issue.

Most Christians feel OK about singing our national anthem, "The Star Spangled Banner." They don't see demons flying around when they sing it; instead, the song stirs deep patriotic feelings.

And maybe the song means more to me than to most Americans, because Frances Scott Key is one of my direct ancestors. Key wrote the words to the song in a poem called "The Defense of Fort McHenry."

But he didn't write the music. That came from John Stafford Smith, a British man. And Smith didn't write that music specifically for Key's words—in fact, he wrote it for a British drinking song. The tune became popular in pubs all over England.

It may seem inappropriate for us to sing about the land of the free and home of the brave to a melody written for a bunch of people drinking in bars all across England—especially since England happened to be our national enemy at the time. Yet the same melody brings tears to our eyes and stirs our patriotism because Key's words gave that British drinking song an entirely new meaning to us. The music is just a vehicle used to communicate an idea.

Martin Luther, the Protestant reformer, was a great songwriter and theologian; he understood this concept well. Luther wrote the words for some of our greatest hymns, but he borrowed the music from popular German folk songs. As a result, people had no problem learning Luther's hymns because they already knew the music. When we sing those hymns today we aren't aware of the origin of the music. It just sounds like "hymn music" to us.

Many of our greatest hymn writers have used the popular, secular music of their day for their hymn lyrics. Bernard of Clairvoux, a 12th-century Christian, set the words of "O Sacred Head Now Wounded" to the tune of a German jig.

Apparently, the writer of many of the Psalms did the same thing. Look at the instructions before Psalm 56 ("To the tune of 'A Dove on Distant Oaks'") and Psalm 57, 58 and 59 ("To the tune of 'Do Not Destroy'"). These instructions to the "song leader" of the day tell him which current tune serves as good accompaniment for this psalm. The origin of the melody is irrelevant; it is the message that is carried by the music that is important.

"Secular" and "Sacred"?

I hope I haven't ruined "The Star Spangled Banner" or some of your favorite hymns by telling you where their music came from. Maybe you can tolerate the use of secular melodies for sacred songs.

But what about secular music that isn't used for any sacred purpose at all? What about plain old "pop" music—the popular music of our own day? Is it all right for Christians to listen to and enjoy songs that are not written by Christians and have no religious or patriotic purpose?

Once Jimmy Swaggart, an outspoken critic of popular music, appeared on "The 700 Club," a religious TV show. Someone asked Swaggart what he thought about the song, "White Christmas," a song your parents and grandparents have probably heard Bing Crosby sing for years and years. Swaggart's response was: "The truth is that it's not edifying to the cause of Christ; it does not glorify or lift up Jesus Christ." Therefore, the song was "bad" For Mr. Swaggart, and many others, if a song does not specifically mention Christ or speak in religious jargon it has no value.

In the view of Mr. Swaggart—as well as many other Christians—everything needs to be "sacred." There's no place for the "secular."

This view means there's no place in God's earth for material that doesn't talk about Christ. Songs must be about Jesus. Love poems would disappear—unless the poems were about love for God. Books are only OK if they are about the Bible, Christians, or Christianity. Paintings must portray Jesus, crosses or other religious subjects and themes.

The logical extension of this view is that you could only receive Christian mail from a Christian postal carrier. When the toilet or the sink got clogged up you would need to call a Christian plumber. Your breakfast cereal would probably be "Be of Good Cheer-i-os," and the only tooth-paste you would use would be G.L.E.E.M. (God Loves Everybody, Especially Me)! You would have to buy your car from a Christian auto dealer, and you would be required to put "Honk if you love Jesus" stickers all over the bumpers, fenders, and doors—as well as over all the windows and windshield.

This Is My Father's World

Do you wear eyeglasses or contact lenses? Do they have fishes or crosses on them? If not, please leave them on and read what I'm saying anyway, because it's extremely important.

There is only one thing that separates that which is spiritual from that which is unspiritual. And it's called sin. If there is something sinful in your life, you must throw it away. There is no place in the Christian life for casual tolerance of sin.

But if something is not sinful, it can be used to glorify God, the Creator of all good and beautiful things.

Martin Luther sums it up very well in declaring, "The cobbler praises God when he honestly makes a good pair of shoes." Or, as the old hymn says, "This is my Father's world."

Likewise, the Apostle Paul says, "Whatever you do, work at it with all your heart, as working for the Lord, not for men" (Colossians 3:23). And he says, "Whatever you do, do it all for the glory of God" (1 Corinthians 10:31).

We need to remember that Satan is called the god of this age and the ruler of the world. Satan does have power here. But God is greater, and likewise, greater is the power that is within us. Satan has never created or fathered anything except sin, yet some speak of Lucifer as if he were the creator of music. He is not.

God is the creator of music and of all things. Satan, in his rebellion, has perverted many areas of God's perfect creation, but he has no power to bring into being things which did not previously exist. He can only rearrange, taint or pervert that which God has already created. And that is his strategy concerning modern music.

Satan has invaded many areas of communication and art today: music, television, movies, books, and radio. And he would love to claim all of these as his own creations. The good news is that these areas are God's first. And if Satan has temporarily claimed them, we can reclaim them and return them to the service of the Creator!

Eddie and I don't worship rock and roll. We don't think it's good or bad. We do like it, and we know many other people do as well. And we use it as a tool to convey the healing, saving message of Christ.

How Will You Use Your Tools?

So what do I say when someone asks me if rock music is a tool of Satan or a tool of God? I say, "Yes. It's both." So are many other things in this world.

The important thing to remember is that it's up to us to use the tools God has given us. We can use the telephone to bring good cheer or make obscene phone calls. We can use music to bless or condemn. And we can use our eyes, ears, and mind to take in things that are bad or things that are good. It's up to us.

And don't forget: Your life is a "tool," too. God has given you that life along with many talents and gifts, and you can use these gifts to serve God and man or you can use them to hurt. It's up to you.

Tool of Satan or Tool of God?

CHRISTIAN
HEROES

I was 15 years old, and it was my very first rock concert—Jimi Hendrix live in Memphis.

When I arrived at the auditorium the atmosphere was charged with electricity, excitement and anticipation. I stood with mouth and eyes wide open, scanning the band's huge wall of amps and speakers, until suddenly Hendrix, clothed in a multicolored cape and with scarves flowing from his head, took the stage.

The crowd went crazy with applause. But the applause was soon drowned out by a wave of sound that poured from the amps. The lights burned like the noonday sun; all eyes were focused on Hendrix as he played—or wrestled with—his guitar, pulling sounds from the instrument like it was some wailing electronic beast.

After what seemed like only an instant—but was really more than an hour and a half—Hendrix tossed his guitar over his shoulder and said goodnight.

That evening changed my life. I went home, put away my catcher's mitt, and began practicing my guitar like never before. I took down the pictures of sports heroes that had covered the walls of my room, replacing them with posters of Hendrix. I bought all of his albums and laboriously memorized every lyric and every guitar line.

My zeal didn't stop with Hendrix's music. I studied his Eastern-influenced philosophies and adopted as my own his rebellious attitude and seemingly unstoppable experimentation with psychedelic drugs. I didn't realize it at the time, but I was beginning to idolize Hendrix as a supernatural person, almost an anti-establishment messiah.

That illusion was shattered on September 18, 1970, when I heard the news: Hendrix had choked to death on his own vomit as a result of a drug overdose.

With almost poetic irony, the drugs and reckless abandon Hendrix advocated had reached out and strangled my hero to death.

I don't know why, but we all seem to need heroes. When our heroes are well chosen, these people can encourage and inspire us to do something great with our lives. When we choose the wrong types of heroes, our lives can be as twisted and wasted as theirs are.

Maybe it was a blessing in disguise that my hero Jimi Hendrix died, because his death left me asking many questions about the meaning of life that finally brought me to trust Jesus as my Savior. If he had lived, it's possible that my illusion would have continued—along with my own experimentation with drugs. Maybe it would have been me who died, choking on my own vomit. But somehow, by God's grace I was spared.

Looking back at those years fills me with fear. I was an ordinary kid from a good home with Christian parents who loved me, yet I was somehow seduced into believing that a talented and charismatic guitarist could give my life purpose and hope. What scares me is that I didn't realize what an important fixture Hendrix had become in my life. I didn't see that I had become so lonely and hungry for something or someone to hang my hopes on that I latched onto an amazing but ultimately doomed guitar player.

Hendrix is dead. But every day brings a new hero into the spotlight. Rock stars are still the prime source of hero material for many, as they were for me. Others find their heroes in movies, in professional sports, daytime soap operas, or even street gangs or adult magazines.

Some of today's youth heroes are healthy and positive—but many of them are dangerous, and they're infecting the hearts and minds of millions of kids with their warped and deviate lifestyles. Without knowing it, many young people are having their lives turned around—in the wrong direction—by these undeserving heroes.

Through the years I've gotten to know some of today's "rock heroes" offstage, and I've found that much of what they say and do is strictly "show biz." They have a carefully crafted image that makes them look tough, daring and a little frightening. But their real lives are normal—even boring!

Unfortunately, by the time some kids are old enough to

distinguish the show biz trappings from the real thing, it's too late. They've already been deeply affected and perhaps even permanently scarred by their heroes.

The Need for Heroes

Don't get me wrong. I'm not saying it's wrong for kids to have heroes. What I'm saying is this: It's wrong for them to turn their heroes into idols (like I did with Hendrix); and it's wrong for them to have the wrong heroes.

Let's look at the difference between heroes and idols. Webster's defines a hero as "a man admired for his courage, fortitude, prowess, nobility." There are two important things that set heroes apart from idols. The first is the word "man"—which doesn't mean that a hero has to be a male instead of a female. Rather, it means that a hero is a human, with human limitations and frailties, instead of a god of some kind. The second is the word "admiration." A hero is not someone who is worshiped; he is someone who is respected.

Compare this to Webster's definition of an idol: "an image of deity used as an object of worship." An idol is someone or something that is revered as more than human. An idol is godlike, worshiped rather than respected.

My esteem for Jimi Hendrix got out of hand when it became idolatry—when I began to believe that Hendrix was more than human. Because of his unbelievable talent and his charismatic charm I felt he must be in some way above the rest of us mere mortals. But his horrible death woke me out of my dream state.

Christian Heroes—
the Good, the Bad, and the Ugly

I'm not trying to pick on Jimi Hendrix. *All* people—including the celebrities of stage and pulpit—have their faults. It would be easy for me personally to pretend that *I* don't have any; all I would have to do is hide behind my

Christian Heroes

stage persona and keep people at a safe distance. But my wife, my children, and the guys in the band who see me day in and day out know I have my faults.

And I'm not the only one. In the last few years we've seen how some big-name Christian leaders have fallen. What can we learn from that? That we all sin and fall short of God's glory, and that we all need to face up to our shortcomings and let people know we are merely sinners in need of God's grace.

I'm not saying that there needs to be a press release every time a Christian leader loses his temper or has bad breath; but there are plenty of appropriate public opportunities when artists like Eddie and me, as well as others, can make it clear that we are only human and that we're just as dependent upon our Savior for his mercy and strength as everyone else.

When I first read my Bible as a new Christian, one of the things that really strengthened and comforted me was that God, in his wisdom, saw fit to include both the good and the bad about the heroes of Scripture. How intimidating it would have been to hear the men of the Bible say, "Be ye holy," if we believed this command came from people who had perfectly mastered holiness. How comforting it is to know that even the righteous man falls seven times—but rises again.

How welcome Paul's words in the book of Romans were to me as a young Christian: "I know that nothing good lives in me, that is, in my sinful nature. For I have the desire to do what is good, but I cannot carry it out. For what I do is not the good I want to do; no, the evil I do not want to do— this I keep on doing." Paul seems to scream out: "What a wretched man I am! Who will rescue me from this body of death? Thanks be to God—through Jesus Christ our Lord" (Romans 7:18,19,24,25).

There are many times in my Christian life that I can relate to Paul's scream. Having faults, sins and weaknesses is a part of every Christian's everyday life—and that includes me. It also includes all of our Christian leaders.

Some Christians try to deny their faults, but it's impossible to be faultless—unless you are God. And any leader who claims to have no faults makes himself a deity—while making others feel weak and hopeless.

For most of us, covering up our human frailty is impossible. But in this age of media hype and Hollywood gimmicks, hiding from one's own sinfulness is both possible and tempting. I know it has tempted me. But that's why leaders and entertainers and other Christians who are in the public eye need to be honest with others about their shortcomings.

We all need to see Christian leaders who remain humble, who are in the spotlight yet publicly admit their weakness and their dependence upon Christ. If more of us in positions of visibility and responsibility did this, the body of Christ would be stronger—and more honest about its own faults.

Heroes of the Faith

People become what they look up to. Before Hendrix died I was trying to become more like him, both in his musicianship and in his lifestyle.

A few years ago, 4,000 high school students were asked to name their heroes. Four of the top eight names were secular rock stars: Prince, Madonna, Bruce Springsteen, and Eddie Van Halen. Some of the adults I've told about this survey get angry. "Why do these kids respect these rock stars?" they ask. "Why don't they look to Christ instead of these phony, secular heroes?"

It's true that there are real dangers in elevating any human being to a position of respect and honor. But there is a clear biblical place for following good examples and a real need for Christian heroes in all of our lives. Young people, especially, need heroes. And the Bible gives us plenty of examples of heroes we should respect and follow. That's why Christian bookstores are filled with the biographies of great saints.

The author of the book of Hebrews agrees with me.

This book contains a kind of "who's who" list of faith heroes. The roster begins in chapter 11, verse 2. In this list we find such great names as Abraham, Rahab, Joseph, Samson and David. Then, at the end of this great list of faith heroes, the author says, "Therefore, since we are surrounded by such a great cloud of witnesses, let us throw off everything that hinders and the sin that so easily entangles, and let us run with perseverance the race marked out for us" (Hebrews 12:1).

The author never intended for us to worship these great men and women, but rather to regard them as role models. They are spiritual pacesetters—heroes of the faith—who have set an example which we are to follow.

If the author of Hebrews were writing today, he might add some names that are more familiar to us: Martin Luther, John Calvin, C.S. Lewis—or maybe even Billy Graham, or Mother Theresa, or Christian recording artist Keith Green. The author of Hebrews wasn't trying to create Christian celebrities or to lead us into idol worship. He was trying to give us a list of real live human role models—along with their deeds—to inspire us to Christlikeness.

The heroes listed in Hebrews include "religious" workers, but "secular" folks are there as well—like Abel the farmer, Sarah the housewife, and David, who before becoming King of Israel was a professional musician (I Samuel 16:16-19). Likewise, today's faith heroes can come from any occupation or field, including music and entertainment. Yet being on stage or in front of a camera is not what qualifies one as a Christian hero. The only qualification is a life of faith and devotion to Christ. In fact, maybe you can be a hero!

God, Our Only Real Hero

The author of Hebrews recognizes that it's only faith in God that makes one a hero, and he wisely begins and ends his list with the mention of God. The first great deed of faith mentioned in verse three is God's work of creation: "By faith we understand that the universe was formed at God's command, so that what is seen was not made out of what is visible." He concludes his list with Jesus, the "author and perfector of our faith, who for the joy set before him endured the cross" (Hebrews 12:2).

By placing God at the beginning and at the end of this list of heroes the author is reminding us to keep our divine perspective. When we lose that divine perspective and turn our attention to human heroes, those heroes can become distracting and dangerous.

In Acts, the Apostle Paul skillfully avoided a chance to make himself into a divine superhero. He and his group had gone to the city of Lystra, where Paul performed a miracle of healing during one of his sermons. This ignited his audience: "When the crowd saw what Paul had done, they shouted in the Lycaonian language, 'the Gods have come down to us in human form!' Barnabas they called Zeus, and Paul they called Hermes because he was the chief speaker" (Acts 14:11, 12).

People from the crowd wanted to offer a sacrifice to Paul and Barnabas, but the apostles responded with appropriate Christian humility: "But when the apostles Barnabas and Paul heard of this, they tore their robes and rushed out into the crowd, shouting: 'Men, why are you doing this? We are only men, human like you. We are bringing you good news, telling you to turn from these worthless things to the living God'" (Acts 14:15).

Rather than accepting the crowd's misdirected praise, Paul made every effort to give his audience a divine perspective concerning the miracle that had happened—just as each of us, when we are elevated to a position of celebrity or honor, has the responsibility to remind our audience, "We are only men, human like you." When a Christian hero reaffirms his humanness and redirects the praise to God, he can then become a powerful tool for the kingdom of God, just as Paul was in the city of Lystra.

But with all his humanness, Paul continued to preach and perform miracles in public. And he continued to speak out for the positive benefit of positive faith heroes, even using himself as an example! At one point Paul even makes this bold declaration: "Follow my example" (I Corinthians 11:1). Paul wasn't ashamed of being a Christian role model—he even promoted himself as one. But he wisely added the divine perspective by saying: "Follow my example, as I follow the example of Christ." It is Christlikeness that separates the faith hero from the ordinary hero. It is Christlikeness that is worthy of imitation.

Like the author of Hebrews, Paul never allowed those who revered him to forget the divine perspective and take their eyes off God. Neither should any of our contemporary Christian heroes.

God's Amazing, Ordinary Heroes

It's not just big-name Christians who have a responsibility to be heroes. God's "ordinary" people are called to be heroes as well.

Our job is to live out our faithfulness to God daily, so that people see they don't need a million-dollar smile, a snazzy silk suit, or a fancy electric guitar to be a Christian.

In fact, ordinary Christians often make the best heroes. Celebrities face major challenges when it comes to being disciples of Christ. When I was a young Christian I talked to friends about the huge impact that a big star like Paul McCartney or Bob Dylan could have in God's kingdom if only he would become born again. Several years later, Bob Dylan *did* come to Christ. He was immediately made into a larger-than-life-size Christian celebrity; his words were studied and even memorized as if he had spent years with God, studying Scripture. In reality he was only a baby Christian.

Whether Dylan's highly public Christian experience did good or harm to the kingdom of God we'll never know; but I do feel certain that it was harmful to Dylan to undergo the pressure of being cast as the rock-and-roll apostle overnight.

In the early centuries of the young Christian church, new Christians were sometimes given a one-year waiting period before they could be baptized. It was a testing period, to see whether the new convert intended to stick it out.

I'm not arguing for a one-year waiting period before baptism, but the principle of giving converts a testing period to examine the sincerity of their faith makes sense. My pastor used to say that when a secular celebrity comes to know Christ, he or she should sit in back of the church and listen for at least a year.

Christians don't need overnight sensations. We need heroes who have deep roots in the divine—not merely nice-looking leaves and branches. We don't need Hollywood-packaged heroes who look good on the outside. We need role models that are real human beings with real human frailty—yet are overcomers by the power of God. We don't need another Christian Miss America, or converted pro football player, or talented TV preachers, or even a converted rock star! We need to see people whose lives are a testimony to their faith in Christ.

Choosing--and Following--Good Examples

Christians need heroes, especially Christian young people who receive so many conflicting signals about what kind of people they should look up to. I'm thankful that God led me to some wonderful biographies of Christian heroes when I was young and hungry in my faith. In fact, one of the greatest experiences of my life was when I was in Bible college and I was required to read the biographies of great Christian heroes like D.L. Moody and Hudson Taylor. What a privilege to read about these men just when I was looking for Christian examples after whom I could pattern my own life.

Christian heroes emerge in every age, and they come from a wide range of vocations and walks of life. We will do well to point out to one another those in our midst who are exemplary in faith and devotion to Christ—the pacesetters for all of us who "run with perseverance the race marked out for us" (Hebrews 12:1).

Christian Heroes

ROCK TODAY, HYMNS TOMORROW

It was an unusually cold winter, but the deep snow didn't prevent concerned religious leaders from all over the country from attending this meeting to debate the latest controversial figure in Christianity. The people were moody, the atmosphere tense—but all seemed to agree on one thing: they denounced the man's questionable theology and revolting music. Their verdict was final. The man was a heretic, and his music—"Well, it has probably damned more souls to hell than his theology."

Who could this man be?

Maybe Glenn Kaiser, leader of Rez Band and one of the elders in a radical Christian community in Chicago called Jesus People USA?

Or maybe Robert Sweet, spokesman and drummer for Stryper, the band that believes God can use hard rock and spandex?

Or maybe Eddie and I being called before another meeting of elders in our church?

Nope. It was none of these modern folks. The man being condemned was Martin Luther, the father of the Protestant Reformation.

What was the problem with his theology? It was his "new" teaching of justification by faith that upset the Council of Cardinals.

What was wrong with his music? He had taken popular German drinking songs and substituted Christian lyrics for the original words. To the Cardinals, Luther's music was proof that he was influenced by the Devil. But today we regard his hymn, "A Mighty Fortress Is Our God," as a classic of the faith.

What can we learn from this angry meeting? In what ways is today's church like that gathering of Cardinals? And how can we as followers of Christ separate the good from the bad in all the new things that come down the pike?

400 Years of Musical Disharmony

In 1988 *Contemporary Christian Music Magazine* celebrated its tenth anniversary. As part of their celebration they asked some of their regular writers and music critics to choose the best Christian albums of all time. The critics' choice was clear: they chose Larry Norman's classic album, "Only Visiting This Planet."

I remember when I first got that record. Inside the album on the record sleeve was "The Story of Solid Rock," an essay Norman had written in 1975 about the purpose of his record company. In that essay, Norman discussed the evolution of Christian music over the past 400 years.

He began with Martin Luther who, as we have seen, was criticized in the 1500s for his novel music and then revolutionary theology. Then came Isaac Watts, who as a young man in 1690 grew bored with the hymns of his day. His father got tired of Isaac's complaining, and challenged his son: "If you think you can write better hymns, then why don't you?" Watts accepted his father's challenge, and wrote more than 350 hymns, including "When I Survey the Wondrous Cross."

Finally, Norman discussed William Booth. Booth's sin was replacing standard church instruments like the piano and organ with trombones, trumpets, tubas, tambourines and drums. He took this big marching Salvation Army brass band out onto the streets and played for the unsaved.

During the last 20 or 30 years we've seen plenty of arguing in the church about music. But Christians have been arguing about music for at least four centuries. Since Martin Luther's day, if not before, music has been a great source of disharmony in the church. But even though the styles of music have changed over the years, the way Christians deal with change has been the same for centuries.

The Church's Acceptance Cycle

I learn a lot from my kids. Just when they get used to their standard set of toys and things, my wife Anita and I get them something new—and it takes them a while to adjust to it.

The church is the same way. Everything that is new—whether it is a new idea, a new song, a new invention, a new translation of the Bible, or a new style of choir robes—must work its way through something I call the *Church's Acceptance Cycle.*

Here's how the cycle works:

Step One: Fear and Loathing. Any New Thing—whatever it is—is greeted with fear and skepticism. Every nuance of the New Thing is thoroughly debated, discussed, examined and scrutinized. After all that, the New Thing is usually completely rejected.

Step Two: Reconsideration. No matter how badly the New Thing is hated in Step One, there will be some who recognize its value. If these people are particularly brave and secure in their faith they may even speak up about the good they see in the New Thing.

Naturally, these pioneers cause quite a stir. There is more debate, and these folks may lose their friends. If things are really bad, they get rocks thrown through their windows or they get run out of town. At the end of Step Two, people are a little bloodier—but the New Thing is one step closer to home.

Step Three: Acceptance. Finally, the New Thing which everyone previously thought of as foolish, inappropriate, and maybe even demonic, becomes generally accepted and regarded as wholesome. That which was once controversial becomes—slowly but surely—part of the status quo. Everyone agrees what a wonderful object the New Thing is. And many of the New Thing's former critics are busy patting themselves on the back.

Step Four: Stagnation. The final step on the Church Acceptance Cycle is, unfortunately, stagnation. The New Thing is no longer debated—or even thought of. In fact, the New Thing is now just another Old Thing. Everyone now assumes that this Thing was always with us, and they can't imagine how life was before the Thing. The Thing which once was new, exciting and provocative is now just another piece of the church's woodwork.

Step Five: Start Over. Now other people are busy coming up with other New Things, and the process starts all over.

God Says "Check It Out"

Does it sound like I'm critical of the Church's Acceptance Cycle, or that I think it's cumbersome or unnecessary?
Believe me, that's not true—even though it has sometimes
been used against Eddie and myself for over a decade. In
fact, I believe the Church's Acceptance Cycle is not only a
good idea, but also clearly Scriptural. Just look at what Paul
said to the Christians in Thessolonica: "Test everything.
Hold on to the good" (1 Thessalonians 5:21).

Or listen to what John wrote in one of his letters: "Dear
friends, do not believe every spirit, but test the spirits to see
whether they are from God, because many false prophets
have gone out into the world" (I John 4:1).

Or look at what Paul wrote to Timothy: "For everything God created is good, and nothing is to be rejected if it
is received with thanksgiving, because it is consecrated by
the word of God and prayer" (I Timothy 4:4-5).

I could cite more verses, but the idea is clear. God
obviously wants us to carefully examine all New Things
before we accept them into our lives or into the life of his
Church—which he has called to be a pure and spotless
bride.

Why does God want us to be so careful? Because there
are three invaders from which we must constantly protect
ourselves: the world, the flesh, and the Devil. The Church
Acceptance Cycle is a wonderful way to defend against
these three spiritual invaders. Just as the white blood cells
of our physical body attack harmful foreign invaders, so the
body of Christ has its defensive system against evil invaders.

What this means is that some of those conservative
folks you might have thought of as "old fuddy duds"—you
know, the ones who resist any and every form of change—
may be doing the will of God and serving a useful purpose!
So instead of grumbling when older (and usually wiser)
Christian brothers and sisters express doubts about the

latest trend to sweep the church, thank God that he has established a system to protect his children. And learn yourself how you can more carefully discriminate between those things which are harmful and those things which are helpful.

Weighing Contemporary Christian Music

Christian songwriters and musicians are not exempt from the Church Acceptance Cycle, and every Christian songwriter—from Martin Luther to Bill Gaither—has seen his work carefully examined before it found general acceptance in the body of Christ.

As for contemporary Christian music, it is now somewhere between the second the third stages of the Acceptance Cycle. Although there is still a great deal of debate over its value in some circles, contemporary Christian music has been adopted by many others. And someday it will no doubt become part of the status quo in your area, if it hasn't already. Maybe someday the debate and arguing over contemporary Christian music will stop altogether, and this new music will become part of the church's life. But by then, of course, we'll be busy debating some other New Thing.

I've seen the effect the Church Acceptance Cycle has had on DeGarmo & Key's music. When Eddie and I began playing over a decade ago, we were considered extreme and radical. As the years go by, our music moves more and more to the mainstream of Christian music, and it's gaining acceptance.

One measure of that acceptance is that Bill Gaither and Sandi Patti have recorded our song, "Blessed Messiah." Another measure is that many church choirs now sing our music on Sunday mornings, right alongside hymns by other "radicals" like Luther and Watts. Among the DeGarmo & Key songs that have been published in hymnals and songbooks are "In His Love," "Alleluia, Christ is Coming," "Let the Whole World Sing," "Destined to Win," and "When the Son Begins to Reign." I get goosebumps hearing a choir sing our songs, and I thank God that he has led people to the point where they can enjoy these songs along with the classic songs of the faith.

And it's not just DeGarmo & Key's songs that have become "hymns." Hymnbooks now contain many songs from the Jesus movement, tons of songs by Bill and Gloria Gaither, as well as songs like "El Shaddai" (written by Michael Card and popularized by Amy Grant) and "Easter Song," by the Second Chapter of Acts.

Squeezing the Fruit

Have you ever seen somebody shopping for fruit and vegetables in the grocery store? My mom's procedure was to look around until she saw a piece of fruit she liked. But she knew she couldn't trust her eyes, because an apple or tomato that looked good on the outside might be rotten on the inside. So she would squeeze it to see how firm it was. Or if it was a watermelon, she would knock on it with her knuckles, listening to see how ripe it was.

Whether they know it or not, people who shop for produce like my mom did are following a profound and important teaching of Jesus: "'Watch out for false prophets. They come to you in sheep's clothing, but inwardly they are ferocious wolves. By their fruit you will recognize them. Do people pick grapes from thornbushes, or figs from thistles? Likewise every good tree bears good fruit, but a bad tree bears bad fruit'" (Matthew 7:15-17).

In the early 70s, contemporary Christian music was too young a tree for people to know what kind of fruit it would bear. Many had a "wait and see" attitude before endorsing or rejecting it. Now, I believe, the verdict is in—and the fruit of contemporary Christian music has been good and bountiful. In the DeGarmo & Key ministry alone we have seen more than 10,000 decisions for Christ in the past two years, including first-time decisions to accept Christ as well as decisions made about vocations. Many of those people have written our office telling us they that they're going on to be pastors, missionaries or Christian musicians. I've read the letters, and I've talked to these people. I know God has used our music as part of his plan, and I'm thankful.

Like Paul, who attributed miracles he performed to God, we give God the credit for any decision made for him at any of our concerts. But we've tried to give God plenty of chances to work through our ministry. We have never given a concert in which we didn't challenge Christians and non-Christians to holiness and to devotion to Christ Jesus as Lord. We talk about sin, and we offer the simple gospel as the only remedy—and people all over the world are responding, because Jesus is being lifted up.

I'm not defending every musical group that calls itself a contemporary Christian music ministry. Some walk with the Lord and do his will; others don't. It's as simple as that. Every minister and ministry must be evaluated individually.

But as time passes and as the Church Acceptance Cycle works on contemporary Christian artists, each ministry will be judged on the basis of the fruit produced. The fruit of contemporary Christian music in general has been and still is very good.

The Church Acceptance Cycle—our fruit inspection process—is slow-moving and sometimes trying for those of us who love contemporary Christian music. But we must keep in mind that this process is both healthy and clearly biblical. And God is using it to produce good fruit in all areas of the church.

CHAPTER

9

COMING
TO DIE

I was working late one night in the recording studio. About 2 a.m., I fixed myself a cup of black coffee and sat down in the middle of a group of engineers and musicians who had congregated in the studio lobby.

As will often happen when you get a bunch of guys together late at night, everyone was telling stories. As I sat down, a talented secular musician named Don Nix was taking his turn at dazzling the tired group.

Don wore the hat he had worn as an elite Green Beret soldier. But Don's beret sat upon a decidedly nonmilitary-looking crop of shoulder-length hair. Don also wore his reputation—that of being an all-around tough guy. It was rumored that he carried a compact Israeli machine gun under the seat of his car.

Don was telling about his days with the Green Berets, and how his rigorous training had prepared him—both mentally and physically—to seek and destroy the enemy behind their own lines.

In Vietnam, Don's group of soldiers had been joined by a team of specially-trained South Koreans. The Koreans, though small in stature, were known as some of the fiercest fighting men in the world. They were often sent to the places where the fighting was the worst, but despite a high casualty rate they never showed fear. They fought with reckless abandon. And instead of wearing green berets, the unique thing about the Koreans' uniforms was that they each wore a black arm band.

After fighting alongside these Korean soldiers, Don finally asked one of them about the black arm bands. The Korean looked at his arm band, and then looked at Don. He told Don his own terrible story of pain and struggle; like most of the the other men in this South Korean fighting unit, he had lost family, friends, and possessions to communism. These men had resolved to give their lives in order to stop the spread of communism in Southeast Asia, and the arm bands were the outward symbols of their commitment.

"This arm band means that I've come to die," said the Korean soldier. And Don saw that these men had faced life

Dana and
bass player,
Tommy Cathey
during rehearsal
prior to shooting
Rock Solid...
the Rock-u-ment

*and death squarely. They had made their commitment.
They no longer had anything to fear.*

They had come to die.

The Heart of the Matter

David Wilkerson delivers a blistering attack on Christian rock music in his book *Set the Trumpet to Thy Mouth* (World Challenge, 1985). As part of his criticism, Wilkerson asks a most important question: "What is in the heart of rock lovers and promoters? That is the question God is most concerned with." (p. 107)

I couldn't agree with Wilkerson more! The condition of the heart is truly the critical issue. God is concerned with our hearts, and until our hearts are made pure we can't truly serve God.

Wilkerson is also right about how we Americans make an idol out of our television sets. And I think he's right about the destructive influence of much of secular rock. I appreciate his call to holy living.

But Wilkerson's book is based on a faulty and unfair assumption: that the hearts of all people involved in contemporary Christian music are impure. I know that isn't true.

Over the past ten years it has been my privilege to tour with dozens of Christian artists. Touring isn't the wonderful, glamorous life that most people think it is. Usually, it's a grueling mixture of sleeping on bumpy buses, being away from friends and family members, and eating disagreeable truck-stop food.

But it has its moments, and for me one of the highlights of touring has been travelling with some of the fine Christian musicians we have played with.

Eddie and I choose the people we travel and perform with very carefully. We get to know a band, listen to their music, watch them in concert and talk to them about their Christian walk before we tour with them. We also call their record company, their managers, concert promoters and others who have dealt with them to see what kind of reputation and Christian testimony they have.

I believe in that process. But even when we have played at festivals and other places with artists we've not subjected to that kind of scrutiny, I can honestly say that we have never met any Christian performers who were not deeply committed.

We have toured with a dozen or more artists over the years—people like Rez Band, Servant, Petra, Mylon LeFevre, Jessy Dixon, the Altar Boys and others—and while we have travelled we have spent a great deal of time in prayer and in Bible study. We've gotten to know where they stand spiritually.

All of these artists can testify to a clear salvation experience, and most of them to something else—a time of breaking. Many describe a trip to the wilderness like Christ's period of testing in the desert. This period of cross-examination by the Holy Spirit seems to produce a fruitful ministry.

Experiences like this have many names—breaking, dying to self, the dark night of the soul, and others. For me, it was a period of breaking; God broke me inside and took away my desires for anything but his will. Let me tell you about it.

Coming to Die

Brokenness by God's Firm but Gentle Hand

It was in the Spring of 1977, and it had been a rough week. Eddie and I had been getting some criticism about our unusual style of Christian rock, and we had been doing some real soul searching. We were asking God, "Can our talents be used by you?"

One afternoon I reached my limit. I came home and hurled my electric guitar into the closet. I got down on my knees before the Lord and finally let go of my dream of being a rock star.

I told the Lord that I was sick of playing God—that I wanted *him* to be God. I was tired of trying to plan my own future and make my own dreams come true.

For the first time ever in my Christian experience, I was able to tell the Lord with sincerity that what I wanted most was to know and serve him. I offered him my body as a servant—and for the first time, I didn't add the condition that he allow me to serve him with an electric guitar. What a beautiful moment it was for me as I witnessed the crucifixion of myself!

I rose from my knees a free man—no longer bound by the chains of selfish ambition and ego, free to serve God in the way that he chose without fear of failure.

In some ways, I was like the Korean soldiers Don Nix had told me about that night at the recording studio. Like them, I had lost much. Now I was prepared to die. I had no more fear about what would happen to me. I knew I was in God's hands.

Christ Wants Us to Die

What is true in physical warfare is equally true in the realm of spiritual warfare. If we mean business, we must come to die.

Jesus bids us to come and die. Didn't he tell his followers, "Take up your cross and follow me"? Two thousand years have passed since he said that, and the passage of time has made it hard for us to understand what a radical statement that was. But when he said it, his disciples could look up and see there, on the top of the hill, the tortured bodies of those who had been crucified. For them, the meaning of taking up one's cross was clear—death.

Jesus insists on our total commitment. He is asking for the ultimate sacrifice: our lives. As he said, "Anyone who does not carry his cross and follow me cannot be my disciple" (Luke 14:27).

Following Christ requires the death of our stubborn will, the death of our hopeless attempts to fulfill our lusts and desires—in short, the death of our attempts to play God. The death of self allows nothing to be placed before Christ in our affections: "If anyone comes to me and does not hate his father and mother, his wife and children, his brothers and sisters—yes, even his own life—he cannot be my disciple" (Luke 14:26).

The death of self is painful but necessary if we are to be used by God to expand his Kingdom. Every Christian must endure it if he desires to be fruitful—particularly those in positions of leadership or prominence. That includes missionaries, preachers, teachers—and even Christian rockers!

Death Before Life, Humility Before Honor

I am pleased to report to the world that the vast majority of the contemporary Christian performers we know openly tell of their persistent, onward struggle to keep selfish ambition on the cross. Perhaps this is the key that explains why some of these artists' ministries have been so successful as tools for evangelism.

All around us we see artists with a fearless, no-turning-back style of ministry. And we have watched as the lives of many thousands of people have been changed. Christian rock has reached into dark corners where the church could not go, and as a result kids have been rescued from a world that would gladly chew them up and spit them out again.

Scripture and reason tell us that only one thing can

Coming to Die

account for such fruit—these laborers' hearts must truly be in tune with Christ.

Are You Ready to Die?

That day that I threw my guitar and my music dreams into the closet was the real beginning of God being able to truly use me. As it turned out, he did use my musical abilities. But I gave him the choice.

Let's not try to fool ourselves into thinking we can fool God. He can tell if we are really giving up our desires to do his will. In my case, I left my guitar in the closet for three years and sought other ways to serve God—and as a result, I enjoyed three very productive years with Youth for Christ.

Ultimately, God did give me the desire of my heart by allowing me to play Christian rock music. But I don't think I'd have been trustworthy in such an important subculture ministry until my heart was right with God and I had experienced the death of self.

As Jesus told his disciples, "I tell you the truth, unless

Dana with his mother, Joan, and Josh McDowell backstage at Atlanta Fest, 1988

a kernal of wheat falls to the ground and dies, it remains only a single seed. But if it dies, it produces many seeds'' (John 12:24). I've seen that verse proven true in hundreds of cases—cases where people have been broken by God and than have seen their ministry find its wings, and also cases of barren ministry attempts, filled with frustration and fear and little fruit because the ministers did not die to self.

I encourage you to take your life to Christ and let him break you. It's only when we come to die that we find abundant, full and productive life.

PART

2

WHAT KIND OF MUSIC DOES GOD LIKE?

MUSIC
AND CULTURE

The first time DeGarmo & Key played in Lancaster, Pennsylvania, I fell in love with that place. As we rode into town on the tour bus, I looked out the window, drinking in the beautiful scenery of sleepy farms, rolling hills and seas of grain.

But as soon as we stepped off the bus and into the town, I felt as if I'd traveled back into America's past! Right in front of me were two carriages drawn by horses, traveling right down the middle of the road. The driver and the passengers looked as if they had just been beamed in via time machine from the early 1800s. They wore simple—almost primitive—clothing, and they all seemed to wear long beards and wire-rim glasses.

They looked so out of place on the busy downtown street that my mind raced to find an explanation. Had the local Chamber of Commerce paid these people to dress this way and ride around in buggies in order to promote tourism? Were they on their way to an authentic early American costume party? If so, they would certainly win the prize.

"Dana. Dana. Dana!"

The insistent voice brought me back to reality. It was Tim Landis, our host in Lancaster, asking me, "What's the matter? Haven't you ever seen Amish people before?"

Then I understood. I'd seen these people portrayed in the movie "The Witness." So these were the Amish people. They weren't just play actors in a movie or employees of the local tourism board.

The next day I learned about some of the extreme measures the Amish people take in order to avoid "worldliness." They don't drive cars or tractors. They don't use electricity. Even the Amish carpenters don't use power tools. One Amish couple even bought a new house and immediately tore out the "worldly" fixtures like shower stalls and electrical outlets!

Although I couldn't help but respect their commitment and sincerity, I wondered if they hadn't misunderstood what God means by "worldliness." "What world," I asked myself, "are these people in?"

Music and Culture

In the World, Not of It

The Christian life is full of challenges and trials, questions and issues. One big issue that has challenged Christians for 2,000 years is the issue of how we relate to the world.

Christ explained it to us, but his words are subject to many interpretations: "My prayer is not that you take them out of the world," Christ prayed, "but that you protect them from the evil one. They are not of the world, even as I am not of it" (John 17:15-16).

What did Christ mean? How are we to be "in the world, but not of it"?

Christ and Culture

What would Jesus look like if he came back today? Would he wear a robe and sandals, like he did when he walked the earth? Or would he update his wardrobe? If so, would he wear a nice three-piece suit, or would he wear blue jeans and a leather jacket? Would Jesus come back as a Republican or Democrat? American or Russian?

These aren't idle questions. The way you answer them says a lot about how you look at the complex theological issue of Christ and culture. Basically, the issue is: How does God look at our culture of clothes, lifestyles, and customs?

The Amish people of Pennsylvania have obviously done a lot of thinking about Christ and culture. So have most missionaries. In fact, I first started thinking about Christ and culture at Bible college with my professor, Paul Davidson, who had served half his life as a missionary in Brazil. I can still vividly remember Dr. Davidson saying, "Don't expect others to accept your culture. You only want them to accept your Savior."

Dr. Davidson understood that we are not promoting a particular brand of politics, clothing, music or culture. We are only communicating Christ. He told us to avoid preaching "an ethnocentric gospel," or a picture of Christianity that is based on our own ethnic, racial or cultural biases.

Hudson Taylor's Cross-Cultural Crusade

It was also at Bible college that a man named Hudson Taylor became one of my heroes. Taylor lived in the last half of the 1800s, and is credited with founding the China Inland Mission, which took the gospel to the then-unreached people of China.

What I respected about Taylor—and the thing that sets his life and work apart from other missionaries—was his unique, unorthodox approach to culture. While other missionaries maintained their American customs and dress, Taylor decided he would adopt Chinese customs. He began to dress, look and talk as if he were truly Chinese. He couldn't have cared less about exporting his western culture to China. His only desire was to win the respect and confidence of the people he lived with and to have an opportunity to communicate Christ to them.

It worked. While other missionaries in China were writing home in despair, reporting that the people were hopelessly embroiled in their pagan religion, Taylor happily wrote home to report great victories for Christ in China. Taylor, who had reached a common cultural ground with the people around him, was able to convert thousands to faith in Christ.

Many of Taylor's peers criticized him, but as a proverb says, "Wisdom is justified by her deeds." Taylor not only saw thousands come to know Christ as Savior, but also left an example to those who desire to invade a seemingly impenetrable culture for Christ.

Christ and Cacophony

Imagine this scenario:

It's Sunday morning. The preacher has prepared a sermon, complete with three points and a poem. His tie is perfectly tied and his heart is in tune with the Lord. He's ready to preach—but first, some music.

Then it begins. Cacophony! Banging drums, crashing cymbals, and the twang of strangely tuned guitars.

All the sounds that make up a good preacher's worst nightmare, right? You might ask, "Who let this rock band into the sanctuary?" But this was no rock band. It was a group of Tamil Christians in the country of India, having a normal worship service with instruments that are familiar to them. And the result is sincere worship of God from the heart.

That story was told by Christian rock critic Bob Larson, as he described the culture shock that gripped him while he was preaching in India. But Larson clearly understood that even though the sounds were unfamiliar to his western ears, they constituted unadulterated praise to his Lord: "Their song service was a shock to my system. The banging of drums mingling with a variety of cymbals and untuned guitars sounded like pure cacophony to me. But the smiles on their faces radiated a love for Christ that transcended our dissimilar upbringing."

Larson could see the sincere praise his Indian brothers and sisters were giving to God, even though the cultural package was significantly different from any he had previously experienced.

Being All Things to All Men

Thinking about the experiences of Hudson Taylor and Bob Larson makes me remember something the Apostle Paul wrote to the Jews about Christ and culture: "To the Jews I became like a Jew, to win the Jews. To those under the law I became like one under the law (though I myself am not under the law), so as to win those under the law. . . . To the weak I became weak, to win the weak. I have become all things to all men so that by all possible means I might save some" (I Corinthians 9:20-22).

What does it mean when Paul says he has "become all things to all men"? Does that mean that, in Hudson Taylor's situation in China, he would wear a kimono and eat squid and rice with soy sauce?

Or if Paul were trying to reach Donald Trump or some other important business leader, would he wear a nicely tailored three-piece suit, and maybe spend some time brushing up by reading *Forbes* or *Business Week?*

What if Paul were trying to witness to farmers. Would he wear blue denim overalls and try to study up by reading *The Farmer's Almanac?*

Yes—I think that's just what it means.

Rock and Roll Missionaries

All the things we've been saying about Hudson Taylor in China and Paul in the first century can be applied to those today who struggle to reach the American youth subculture.

That subculture has its own vocabulary, fashions, customs and music, and if you're going to reach those young people for Christ you're going to have to go where they are and speak to them in a language and style they can understand.

That's what DeGarmo & Key and other music ministries are doing. And, even though some may find this surprising, I believe that many of the contemporary Christian music ministries of today will someday be given the same admiration and respect accorded to Christian pioneers such as Hudson Taylor.

In the meantime, Eddie and I—as well as others in our band and other Christian artists—will continue to receive criticism and persecution from some and encouragement from others as we pursue our calling as musical missionaries. We may not be far, far away in distant China bringing the gospel to the Asian masses. And we may not be in the first century with Paul taking the message of the gospel to Jews. But we are communicating Christ's message to the American youth subculture right in front of our noses.

These kids deserve to hear about the Jesus who died for them. And every night when we take the stage, God, who sees our hearts, knows whether we (as well as any other ministers, musical or not) are acting out of devotion and allegiance to him.

KINGDOM OF
THE CLONES

Our band was in the middle of a European tour, on our way to our last date in West Germany. To reach the ancient cathedral in West Berlin where the concert was to be held, we had to travel through communist-controlled East Germany.

I was not prepared for the contrasts.

We had been in West Germany for most of a week and had been amazed at the affluence; Mercedes, Porches, and Volkswagens filled the tree-lined streets of this prosperous-looking nation.

Then we entered communist East Germany. All factories, including auto factories, are state-owned. The automobiles these factories produce are small, dreary-looking two-stroke cars. We were told that it took seven years of waiting on a list to buy one, even though it hardly seemed worth the wait. The bleak roads were littered with broken-down, abandoned cars.

We saw similar contrasts while touring the Berlin wall, which divides these two countries—and the two halves of Berlin. On the free, Western side, we saw children playing and tourists taking pictures. But then we saw the Eastern side: mine fields, electric fences, armed guards—and machine-gun posts, placed about 100 yards apart and stretching as far as we could see.

Growing up in Memphis I was used to seeing armed men around Millington Naval Base. I'd known that those soldiers wouldn't hurt me. They were there for my protection.

But there was a difference in Berlin. The guards and the military hardware weren't there to prevent an invasion of East Germany—they were there to keep East Germans from escaping into freedom. As we walked along the wall, we saw scores of crosses that marked the places where East Germans had died trying to reach that freedom.

1984 Today

Seeing the contrasts in Berlin made me think of *1984*, the terrifying book by British novelist George Orwell. Winston Smith, the main character in the story, lives in a futuristic society where all thoughts, feelings and activities are controlled by the all-powerful state.

No freedom is allowed—either in thought or action. Ever-present cameras record every move of every citizen. The motto of these fearful, powerless people is, "Big Brother is watching you."

When I first read Orwell's *1984*, I was glad that it was only a novel—that its despairing vision of people under oppression wasn't true. But when I visited Berlin, I realized that in many ways *1984* has come true, that in many places on earth oppression is real. The people of East Berlin aren't being watched by cameras in their rooms, but they've lost their freedom to the all-powerful state.

1984 in the Church

God's love is the most liberating force in the world. But unfortunately, there have been times when some in the church have traded this freedom for the power of oppression. One of the most shocking examples of *1984*-style oppression in the church is the Papal Inquisition of the 13th century, during which many so-called heretics were imprisoned and tortured by the Catholic Church.

Religious oppression didn't stop in the 13th Century. It continues today. And sadly, it's the *Christians*, who should be proclaiming Christ's freedom, who are putting other people in chains.

During the 1960s, during the height of the Jesus Movement, many, many young people—many of them with long hair and hippie lifestyles—were coming to Christ. But some churches were less than enthusiastic about young people from the hippie subculture attending their churches. In fact, I heard about one church where, if a long-haired man walked forward during the invitation, the church leaders wouldn't let him kneel and accept Christ unless he let them cut his hair off right then and there. Short-skirted women had to have an addition hemmed on to their skirts to make them longer before they accepted Christ.

Other stories abound of Christians and church leaders mistaking their own will for God's will, and imposing it on people who disagreed. This is the way things were in Orwell's *1984,* but it's not the way things should be in the Body of Christ!

God Desires Unity, Not Uniformity (And Kingdom People, Not a Kingdom of Clones)

So how *should* things be in the church? Should we hire some communist-style dictators to boss us around and keep us in line—theologically and socially? Should we wear plastic smiley-face masks and act like everything is fine? Should we get rid of our individuality so there are no rough edges to bump up against other people? Should we all just give up?

Not in a million years. God's Kingdom isn't built by fear, accusation and intimidation. That's how a kingdom of clones is created. A kingdom of clones is built and maintained by *uniformity*, which means everyone conforms to what everyone else thinks or believes.

Instead, the Kingdom of God is built and maintained by true Biblical *unity,* which is the power to love one another through all our differences. Uniformity is threatened by diversity, but true Biblical unity is promoted in the kingdom of God by diversity. In fact, Christ's Body requires diversity to operate.

Consider these words spoken by the Apostle Paul: "The body is a unit, though it is made up of many parts; and though all its parts are many, they form one body. So it is with Christ. . . . If they were all one part, where would be the body be?" (1 Corinthians 12:12, 19).

Paul's point is that eyes must have feet and feet must have hands and so on for the body to be whole, functioning, and healthy. No individual member is sufficient by itself, just as no member of the body of Christ has all the spiritual gifts. But, because of that diversity, *unity* is necessary.

If any individual member of the body of Christ *had* all the spiritual gifts, he would be sufficient in himself. That wasn't God's intention, so, instead, God wisely sprinkled his grace through the body of Christ so that we will be unified by our need of each other. God has created unity by diversity and by our mutual dependency.

The problem begins when we become intolerant of diversity. We often tend to prefer those who are like ourselves. Those with similar spiritual gifts begin to clump together, thereby cutting themselves off from the grace that would come from different members of the body with different gifts, and also depriving themselves of opportunities to share the gift that they have.

Listen to what the Bible says about diversity of gifts in the church:

> It was he who gave some to be apostles, some to
> be prophets, some to be evangelists, and some to
> be pastors and teachers, to prepare God's people
> for works of service, so that the body of Christ may
> be built up until we all reach unity in the faith . . . .
> From him the whole body, joined and held to-
> gether by every supporting ligament, grows and
> builds itself up in love, as each part does its work.
> (Ephesians 4:11—16)

That sounds like wisdom. But what do we do instead? We look for gifts that are similar to ours, thereby hindering God's unity which comes through diversity. One church becomes a church full of teachers, another becomes a gathering of evangelists, and another becomes a church of healers and miracle gifts. Rather than encouraging each church to have a fair sprinkling of all the gifts, we pridefully focus on the one that we possess or prefer and then add insult to injury by forming a denomination based on our ignorance.

Let's face it: We're all different. God has given us varying gifts and abilities. And in the same way, we have all grown to like various things: some catsup or mustard, some rock music or Bach.

Because of those God-given differences, we're never going to become carbon copies of each other, so there's no point in trying. Instead, we need to find unity in our diversity. Obviously, this doesn't come naturally to us, so here's something that should help make it easier.

Below is a chart that shows the difference between uniformity and unity. Use it as a tool to help you figure out which is which, and how you can work toward unity with your brothers and sisters in Christ:

UNIFORMITY	UNITY
1. Unified in outward appearance	1. Unified in the heart
2. No common goal or vision necessary	2. Common goal of building up the body in love
3. Appearance of unity maintained by rules or laws	3. Unity through the conviction of the indwelling Holy Spirit
4. Cooperation insured by peer pressure, fear, guilt, alienation	4. Cooperation insured by love

Uniformity is a poor substitute for unity. In the end, those who insist on uniformity become the enemies of real unity. They forget that God created us all wonderfully unique and different. They forget that, while we all possess different personalities, gifts, and abilities—like many pieces of a puzzle—we all fit together in the church to make a beautiful mosaic of Christ.

Our Way Isn't Always Christ's Way

I often wonder whether Jesus is upset with his church and the many people who promote their own ideas as if they were speaking in his name!

We should be helping people develop Christlike character by exhorting them along the lines Paul did in Philippians 4:8: "Whatever is true, whatever is noble, whatever is right . . . think about such things." Instead, there are many self-appointed leaders in the church who demand rigid adherence to their own personal tastes in music, dress and other areas. Their admonition should be: "Whatever I like, whatever I prefer, whatever I was raised to believe is all right . . . think about these things, and nothing else—or else."

Remember the patience Jesus showed to his twelve disciples—one of whom he knew to be an unbeliever. This attitude is summed up well by Paul: "The Lord's servant must not quarrel; instead, he must be kind to everyone, able to teach, not resentful. Those who oppose him he must gently instruct, in the hope that God may grant them repentance leading them to a knowledge of the truth, and that they will come to their senses" (2 Timothy 2:24—26).

Today, some leaders believe that their own personal lifestyles are inspired by God, and that it's their job to bash everybody else into submission. Those leaders have mistaken their cultural prejudices for guidance from the Holy Spirit.

What about fashion? What kind of wardrobe does God prefer? Does he like expensive leather shoes, three-piece silk suits and Rolex watches, or does he like blue jeans and T-shirts? Or does he really care what we're wearing?

Sometimes I think God has a gigantic pair of X-ray glasses that go straight through our clothes and straight to our heart. That's what he cares about. We need to avoid getting lost in disputes about appearance and cultural differences. The Bible must stand above our preferences as the final and only judge of what is sin and what isn't.

In fact, God has shown in the past that dressing out of synch with the prevailing popular customs does not necessarily constitute sin or a sinful attitude. Many of God's prophets dressed weird! John the Baptist wore clothes "made of camel's hair, and he had a leather belt around his waist" (Matthew 3:4). Isaiah, at one point, dressed in nothing at all—going completely naked for three years in order to make his point about impending judgment (Isaiah 20:3).

Isaiah and John the Baptist probably wouldn't make anyone's best-dressed list, and I'm not proposing that Christians go nude to proclaim the gospel. All I'm saying is that God's ways may be different from our ways.

The condition of the heart is what's most important to God, not the external appearance. Jesus said, "That which proceeds out of the heart of man is what defiles the man" (Mark 7:20, King James Version). And in making His point to the Pharisees Christ said, "Woe to you, teachers of the law and Pharisees, you hypocrites! You are like whitewashed tombs, which look beautiful on the outside but on the inside are full of dead men's bones and everything unclean" (Matthew 23:27).

To give too much importance to what a man wears rather than the condition of the heart is out of synch with the divine viewpoint. From Genesis to Revelation, God repeats this message: "Stop judging by mere appearances,

Eddie and Dana rocking on stage in Huntsville, Alabama, Spring 1989

Kingdom of the Clones

and make a right judgment" (John 7:24).

If we place undue importance on people's clothes, makeup and appearance, we may alienate the very people we are trying to reach. I remember my disillusionment when, as a young Christian, I was asked not to wear blue jeans to church. I was confused and angry that such an insignificant thing would matter to God.

Now that I've been saved over ten years, I realize that clothes are not important. If someone told me that, to go to church and worship with other believers, I had to wear a double-knit plaid suit (or even a big white toga), I would do it in a minute. But as a young Christian, criticism of my blue jeans hurt me and caused me to stay out of church altogether for a while.

Unity Means Not Criticizing the Brother You Don't Know

Long-distance criticism of the ministries of other people can hinder the work of the gospel and destroy the unity of Christ.

Not long ago a prominent television evangelist went to his nationwide television audience and criticized the De-Garmo & Key video "Six, Six, Six" for being violent and pagan, and strongly implied that we were not Christians at all. What research had he done? None. He had not seen our video, nor had he ever contacted us or our record company to inquire about the video or our ministry.

Later, in a private meeting with this evangelist, a supporter of our ministry explained the nature of the video and of our ministry. The evangelist conceded to them in private that it had some validity. Unfortunately, those words spoken in private did nothing to mitigate the damage caused by his uninformed public message; neither his words nor the electronic signals that carried them to TVs across the country were retrievable.

And it's true that the shoe is sometimes worn on the other foot. Some critics attack television evangelists with abandon, saying, "They're all in it for the glory and the money." It's easy to be swayed by the misdeeds of a few and mistakenly criticize everyone.

When we are tempted to criticize others with a broad brush, a small degree of Christian sensitivity in expressing these misgivings would be more in keeping with the spirit of Scripture and of brotherhood.

Christ said that before we try to take the splinter out of our brother's eye, we should take the log out of our own—in other words, that before we criticize our brother, we should examine our own life.

Another way to say the same thing can be found in a popular current saying: "Whenever you point your finger at someone else, there are three fingers pointing straight back at you."

Admitting You're Wrong vs. Holding Your Tongue

Back in the early days of DeGarmo & Key, I remember reading the book *The Day the Music Died,* by Bob Larson—one of the earliest, angriest, and most-quoted antirock books around. We constantly ran up against Bob's scathing criticisms of Jesus rock as they were relayed to us by the many people who read his books.

But later, Bob changed his mind about contemporary Christian music. He wrote about that change of heart in his book, *Rock*:

> As the beat of contemporary Christian music grew louder and stronger, voices of dissent were raised; mine was one of them. Quite frankly I saw no hope that an authentic spiritually viable medium of musical expression could come out of such confusion. It didn't seem possible that these gospel artists would ever mellow and mature into composers and singers who would explore themes of depth and commitment worthy of acceptance by the church, but in many ways I was dead wrong.
> I also made another more serious miscalculation; though I may have spoken straightly, I too, was part of a new

generation looking for new ways to make the name of Jesus known. Observations and objections I expressed were designed to purify, not stifle; however, as a young writer I seriously underestimated the prejudiced inertia of the evangelical church. . . .These may sound like strange words coming from one who initially objected to some of the trends that have brought us to this day, but I am more than happy to acknowledge the increasing quality and depth of contemporary Christian musical expression.

I can appreciate anyone who will say, "I was dead wrong." The problem is that the accusation usually makes bigger headlines than the apology.

Several years ago, Billy Graham was accused of having a secret multimillion-dollar bank account hidden in Texas. The accusation made headlines all over the country. It later turned out that the account was set up for Billy Graham by some Texas businessmen and that, in reality, Billy Graham received none of the money personally. No wrongdoing was uncovered—but unfortunately, while the accusation made headlines, the explanation ended up buried in the back pages.

While we who love Dr. Graham and his ministry were willing to wait patiently and dig for the explanation, most people saw only a headline accusing Billy Graham of having a secret multimillion-dollar bank account. The public damage was done.

It's easier to avoid saying accusing things to begin with than it is to retract harmful statements once they're made. My prayer is that we will pray for the unity of the church, and that we will learn to exercise restraint on our tongues when we feel inclined to say something harmful about a brother or sister in Christ.

THE KIND OF MUSIC GOD LIKES

The preacher stormed across the stage—sweat pouring down his face and the pages of his Bible fluttering as he paced.

He pointed out at his audience and screamed into his microphone, "I'm not trying to get you to like the kind of music I like! I just want you to like the kind of music God likes!"

"Amen!" the audience shouted back. "Preach it, brother!"

"Don't listen to me, listen to God! And base your musical tastes on God's musical tastes!"

More amens. More cheers.

"What I'm asking you to do is ask what God thinks about rock music. What I think or what you think is unimportant. But I'm asking you to follow what God thinks. And what does God think about rock music? Does he like its pounding, primitive rhythms? Does he like its screeching, shrieking noises? Does he like the sissies and punks who play the guitars and prance around the stage in skin-tight pants? Does God like their booze guzzling, their drug swallowing and their girl chasing?"

Now the crowd was really going.

"You know what God thinks about all this. He hates it! And you should hate it too."

Then it was time for the offering. So as the preacher's combo began playing a southern gospel version of "In the Garden," I ducked out and headed for my hotel room.

But that sermon had me wondering what kind of music God really does like. Does God like the southern gospel music being played back at the auditorium by the preacher's band? And since southern gospel sounds so much like country music, does that mean God likes country music, too?

Or does God prefer classical music? I've known a lot of Christians who swear by Bach, and Handel, and Beethoven.

Does God like good jazz, or is jazz too jazzy? How about that honky-tonk-style gospel music that they play on some of the Christian TV stations?

Or maybe God likes Gregorian chants. After all, the monks wrote and dedicated that music to him.

But what if God prefers Asian or African music? Then

what will we do?
Lord, help me to know what kind of music you like!

What's God's Style?

Ours is an age full of passionate arguments on many issues. It's interesting to me that Christians of varying opinions all claim to have God's perspective on the issues, or God's five-step procedure to fix the problems, or God's candidates for political offices. Even though music and art are highly subjective, there are still plenty of preachers and teachers around who want to give us all God's view on music. According to them, God has a favorite style of music and they can tell us what it is.

I believe that God lives and speaks to us today. And I even believe that God speaks through his servants—at least part of the time. But I grew up in the 60s and 70s, the decades of false messiahs and spiritualists on the take. Having seen the errors, the falsehood, and the sin that can plague even the best-known Christian leaders, I tend to be a little skeptical. I carefully scrutinize anyone who claims to be God's mouthpiece—especially when it involves music.

And, at least in part, that skepticism is valid. God is not the author of confusion, but today so many teachers, preachers, and evangelists claim his authority and proclaim messages that contradict one another.

When it comes to the kind of music God likes, I suspect that many pronouncements are greatly affected by the personal taste of the preacher. Is it just my imagination, or do most Christian leaders endorse and enjoy Christian music that sounds very much like the music that was popular in the part of the country they grew up in at the time they were young?

Many preachers suggest they have a direct channel to God. And some say that if we all pray we will agree with them on the answer. I wholeheartedly agree that we as Christians should earnestly pray about the music we listen to—as well as all of our sources of entertainment and edification. But I also think that even our prayers are sometimes swayed by cultural bias.

Before you crucify me for saying that, let me propose an experiment. Let's ask a Christian from the Orient, a Christian from Africa, and a Christian from the United States to each select one recording of a song that truly ministers to them. Then bring the three folks together to share their songs. Allow each Christian to hear all three recordings and prayerfully rate them from one to three for their "ministry value." If I were a betting man, I'd bet that each rating sheet would be different, and that at the top of each list would be the song sounding the most "normal" (or least foreign) to each person's ears.

Who Speaks for God?

Does it sound as if I don't believe in prayer, or that I'm skeptical about God communicating to his people today? I believe strongly both in prayer and in God's willingness and ability to communicate with us. But ours is an age full of hundreds and thousands of voices crying out for attention, and it takes wisdom and spiritual insight to sort out the good from the bad, the true from the misguided.

Recently Chuck Colson tackled this thorny subject of people speaking for God in his book, *Who Speaks For God?* In describing the voices coming at us from pulpits, TV screens, and everywhere else, he writes, "Many times they sound as if they have just hung up the phone from talking with God."

In fact, so many people claim to be speaking for God that it might be time to dust off an Old Testament system for dealing with mistaken prophets. In those days, if your prophecy didn't come true, you were dead! Read it for yourself:

> But a prophet who presumes to speak in my name any thing I have not commanded him to say, or a prophet who speaks in the name of other gods, must be put to death. You may say to yourselves, "How can we know when a message has not been spoken by the Lord?" If what a

The Kind of Music God Likes

prophet proclaims in the name of the Lord does not take place or come true, that is a message the Lord has not spoken. That prophet has spoken presumptuously. Do not be afraid of him. (Deuteronomy 18:20-22).

If we started practicing this ancient wisdom, we would see fewer casual prophets who change their tune with the weather. But since there are so many who claim to speak for God today, we need to remind ourselves of the truth expressed by Chuck Colson in his book: "Who speaks for God? He does quite nicely for himself through his holy and infallible word and the quiet obedience of His servants."

And Colson is right. We can turn our ears away from the chorus of self-appointed righteous representatives and turn our hearts to the Bible and the guidance of the Holy Spirit. Only God's word is free from the limitations of personal taste and cultural bias: "For the word of God is living and active. Sharper than any double-edged sword, it penetrates even to dividing soul and spirit, joints and marrow; it judges the thoughts and attitudes of the heart" (Hebrews 4:12).

On my first day of Bible college, I drove onto campus and noticed a sign with these words written in stone: "The entrance of thy word giveth light" (Psalms 119:130). Since that day, those words have been engraved on my heart. Likewise, God wants to engrave his teachings on our hearts, and from his teaching comes the light we need to see through the confusing darkness of the music issue.

God's Command: "Praise the Lord"

What kind of music does God like?

The Bible doesn't contain heaven's top-40 playlist, but it does contain the principles and guidelines we need to find music that is pleasing to the Lord.

Some of the most explicit instructions on music in the Bible are found in the Psalms. There, God tells his people how he wants them to worship him. Now, the Psalms don't specify the *style* of music God likes, but they do tell us about praising him, and we can take our musical cues from these instructions.

God's main point for worship can be found in Psalm 150, which sums it all up in three words: "Praise the Lord!" The Westminster Catechism says that the chief end of man is to glorify God. That should be the goal of our lives—and our music.

How shall we praise him? The answer is found in verse three: "with the sounding of the trumpet, . . . with the harp and lyre [the guitar of the day], . . . with tambourine and dancing."

Whoa! Wait a minute, did he say dancing? Yep. That's what the Bible says. As any junior-high-school kid knows, dancing requires music that is rhythmic and energetic. Unfortunately, many Christians today shy away from any style of music that can be danced to.

The psalm continues: "Praise him with stringed instruments and pipes" (verse 4, KJV). As a teenager that verse confused me. My father plays guitar in a conservative-sounding Southern gospel group called the Havenaires. One time he attempted to accompany the group with an electric guitar, but the people in the church got terribly upset. I remember wondering, "Haven't they read the psalm where it says to 'praise the Lord with stringed instruments?'" Maybe they had forgotten that verse.

The psalm goes on: "Praise him with the clash of cymbals, praise him with resounding cymbals." Imagine this if you can: you walk into church, open the hymn book, and begin singing "Amazing Grace." Suddenly, one of the worshipers leaps from his seat with a righteous jig, pulls a pair of giant marching band cymbals out of nowhere, and begins clanging away with all his might.

Let's face it: Anyone who tried to play cymbals in 99% of the churches in America would be quickly escorted to the door. But he would merely be following God's instructions in Psalms, wouldn't he?

One last thought before we leave Psalm 150. With all

the dancing, stringed instruments and loud cymbals happening, doesn't this picture look a little bit like a rock concert?

God's Other Command: Sing a New Song

Over and over, the psalms tell us to praise God. But there's another idea in a number of psalms. And that is that God wants us to sing a new song to him. Psalm 149 tells us: "Sing to the Lord a new song." Psalm 33:3 says, "Sing to him a new song." Psalm 40:3 tells us: "He put a new song in my mouth."

What does God mean when he says to sing a new song? Does it mean that once we've sung "Amazing Grace" at church we should throw that hymn away and never sing it again? I don't think so—although it is a good idea to include new hymns in our singing at church. Sometimes just singing a new song can inspire our faith.

I believe that God is telling us to keep our relationship with him alive and vital. When was the last time there was a new song of praise and thankfulness in your heart for God? Was it last week, or years ago? God desires us to refresh the springs of our praise for him.

God wants us to sing a new song to him! It's not enough for us to say, "'Amazing Grace' was good enough for the Apostle Paul, so it's going to have to be good enough for me." The good-enough-for-me approach is dangerous—it can lead to a dependence on tradition rather than on a vital, growing relationship with Christ. Ultimately, dependence on tradition breeds empty religion. But the Lord desires our relationship with him to be fresh and new everyday. And naturally, some of our music should be fresh and new as well.

"Spiritual" Doesn't Mean "Preachy"

The New Testament offers many helpful tips on making music that pleases God.

Paul says, "Speak to one another in psalms, hymns and

spiritual songs" (Ephesians 5:19). But what does Paul mean when he says "spiritual songs"? How can we recognize a spiritual song when we hear one? Do we count the number of times it says "Jesus," or the number of verses of Scripture quoted?

No. In fact, not every spiritual song needs to mention the Lord's name. Of course, "praise music" usually mentions the name of God frequently, but not every song is a praise song, and not every song needs to include "God" or "Jesus" to be edifying to Christians.

Does that sound radical? Let's look at the Bible. If every book of the Bible needed to mention "God," we would have to remove the book of Esther, which never once mentions God's name.

We would also have to consider removing the Song of Solomon, which rarely mentions the Lord and has as its primary subject matter love between a man and a woman.

Even the Bible shows us that not everything has to be full of the names of God to be spiritual.

Thank goodness. That means that Christian authors can write about the whole world. That means that a tal-

adicam capturing Dana singing during the "Rock Solid...the Rock-u-mentary" filming

The Kind of Music God Likes

ented Christian writer like C.S. Lewis can write science fiction and literary criticism—as well as great theological treatises.

The same goes for artists and painters. They can paint everything on their canvasses—not only pictures of Christ or other "religious" subjects, but also a breathtaking sunset or a beautiful woman. To skillfully paint a sunset in honor of the One who created the sun glorifies God and edifies those who see it. It need not have a cross painted on the horizon in order for it to praise the Lord. If it is done in devotion to Christ with a pure heart and is done skillfully, it glorifies Christ and has value for the saints.

The same principle applies to the world of music. All songs need not mention the name of God to be beneficial and uplifting to the listener. If the song is written in devotion to Christ with a pure heart and is done skillfully it can be valuable to Christians, even if it contains no blatantly "religious" language.

Think on These Things

If the "religious language" test isn't a sure-fire way to evaluate the goodness of a book of the Bible or a song—how can we tell what's "spiritual" and what's not? How can we follow Paul's command to "sing spiritual songs"?

After all, it's impossible for us to know the motives of authors, painters, and musicians. So how do we measure the value of their work?

One of my favorite measuring rods is Philippians 4:8: "Finally, brothers, whatever is true, whatever is noble, whatever is right, whatever is pure, whatever is lovely, whatever is admirable—if anything is excellent or praiseworthy—think about such things."

We read often in the Bible about how important our hearts are. But our minds are also very, very important to God and to our happiness in life. If you can control a person's thought life, you control the person. Francis Schaeffer once said: "The spiritual battle, the loss or victory is always in the thought world. . . .so this is where true spirituality in the Christian life rests, in the realm of my thought life."

The mind is an amazing thing. It absorbs everything it sees, hears, smells or feels—and it stores up all this information for later use. The brain is our computer, and it's terribly important that we screen what goes into it.

In Bible college, I learned this little poem:

"Sow a thought
Reap an action
Sow an action
Reap a habit
Sow a habit
Reap a character
Sow a character
Reap a destiny."

Our thoughts often lead to actions, and thoughts can come from many places—including lyrics to songs.

Each song carries its own message—its own little sermon. We need to take a hard look at the thoughts we're absorbing. We need to remember what types of things Paul tells us to think about, and we need to find those good things.

Paul tells us to think on those things that are true and noble. To me, "true" means "real." We are bombarded with so many things that are false or imaginary, but we need to focus our minds on what's true and real.

Believe it or not, music's not the only source of false messages today. Many false messages come through advertising. Think of the MasterCard commercial: "MasterCard—so worldly, so welcome." The ad seems to tell us that happiness comes through prestige and materialism. Shouldn't Christians know that this is false? Of course. But unless we remember to think on God's truth when we're confronted with so many myths and lies, we may begin to believe them.

Paul also tells us to dwell on "whatever is pure, . . .

lovely, . . . admirable." Perhaps the biggest challenge to purity we face today is in the area of sexuality. But this isn't new. Just like our culture, Paul's culture was bombarded by sexual enticements. In our music and in our life, we need to dwell on sexual purity.

"Lovely" simply means beautiful or attractive, but here too we need to avoid our society's myths. Can a woman who doesn't look like a fashion model be attractive? God says yes. Just check out Proverbs 31 to see what a beautiful wife is. We need to look past externals to the true, internal source of people's beauty. And "admirable" means something that can be admired. Look at the lives of well-known musicians and speakers, both secular and Christian. Are they admirable? We've seen, in recent years, several Christian personalities that we thought were admirable confess to acts that no one should imitate. In contrast, many lesser-known speakers and servants live out lives of quiet dedication and virtue day after day.

Paul concludes: "If anything is excellent or praiseworthy—think about such things." Some translations use the word "virtuous" in the place of the word "excellent." Either way, God is telling us to have high standards. Paul didn't say, "whatever is mediocre or OK." He's challenging us to excellence.

If something is praiseworthy, that means it is worth recommending to others. Are there some things that you like that you'd rather not tell your friends or your parents about, because you're afraid they won't approve? Maybe you shouldn't dwell on those things. Maybe they aren't really praiseworthy.

This passage of Scripture doesn't give us God's top-10 list of favorite music, but it does tell us the standards that our music and lyrics should meet—as well as our television, movies, books, and other forms of entertainment. In fact, everything we do should conform to this scriptural standard. If what you're doing survives the Philippians 4:8 test, you can rest assured that it is good for your soul.

David, the Dancing Fool

One of my favorite passages in the Bible shows us how God looks at our heart—and not at how we look externally. It's the story of King David and his wife Michal found in II Samuel chapter 6.

Israel had lost the Ark of the Covenant—one of their most important possessions—but now had recovered it. David and others were bringing the ark back to Jerusalem, and the Bible says, "David and the whole house of Israel were celebrating with all their might before the Lord, with songs and with harps, lyres, tambourines, sistrums and cymbals."

It was a day of great rejoicing, and David was overwhelmed by the celebration—as the Bible tells us, "David . . . danced before the Lord with all his might." This was no waltz—it was a hearty, energetic dance.

But apparently, David's wife Michal didn't share her husband's joy. She thought he looked silly. As she looked out the window and saw him dancing, "she despised him in her heart." When David returned home, Michal greeted him with a very sarcastic remark: "How the King of Israel has distinguished himself today!" You can almost feel the ice cubes in her veins.

David didn't get upset or yell at his wife. He made a very simple response: "It was before the Lord," he said. "I will celebrate before the Lord." David didn't care what Michal or other people thought. He was praising God, and God knew his heart. That's all he cared about.

You may not have a wife named Michal, but maybe there's a "Michal" in your church or youth group who criticizes you for the way you worship or the Christian music you listen to. There's no need for you to get defensive or angry. Check your heart, and simply tell your critics: "It is before the Lord, and my heart's right." That's all the justification you need.

It's interesting to me that Scripture adds that "Michal . . . had no children to the day of her death." Remember that the legalistic, judgmental life is often a fruitless life. But you don't need to argue with people who judge you. God will deal with them—and you!

So What Music Does God Like?

We don't have a list of approved songs or artists, but we do have some clear and solid key points. Here they are:

1) God likes music of any style or culture that is played skillfully.

2) God likes lyrics that conform to his own holy standards as set forth in Philippians chapter 4.

3) God desires that the skillful music and the virtuous lyrics be performed unto him with the right motivation—to the honor and glory of his Son Jesus Christ.

Seek God's direction in the music you listen to—or perform. Honor Him in your heart and life, and you'll be on the right track.

Dana
on stage

So Long for Now

Here we are at the end of this book. I hope you've enjoyed it, and I hope you've learned as much from reading it as I have from writing it. My prayer is that somehow God will use this book to bring greater understanding and cooperation among his people.

The book is over—but I still feel like I have a lot more to say. It's the same when Eddie and I finish a concert or a record. We can never squeeze everything in. That's why I'm already working on more books to share with you.

In the meantime, let me leave you with the lyrics from the song that provided the title of this book:

Don't Stop the Music

I love to hear that music
Play it slow or fast
I love that healing message
From the distant past
And if I rearrange it
It remains the same
I'll change the way I say it
But never what I say
The message must remain the same

Don't stop, don't stop the music
You've got to let it play
Don't stop, don't stop the music
Play it in your own way
I hear dissenting voices
Quick to disagree
But I'm on a music mission
They don't bother me
I'll sing the songs that set men free

Don't stop, don't stop the music
You've got to let it play
Don't stop, don't stop the music
Play it in your own way

God bless you!

(By Eddie DeGarmo and Dana Key © copyright 1988 DKB Music/
ASCAP, a division of the ForeFront Communications Group, Inc.)

Epilogue: Liberators and Love

"There is no fear in love. But perfect love drives out
fear."—1 John 4:18

"This is how we know what love is: Jesus Christ laid
down his life for us."—1 John 3:16

*It was just a normal, quiet Thursday evening. Our
family had just sat down for dinner. Nobody knew that that
night, April 4, 1968, would change history.*

*We had turned the television down so we could eat
dinner in peace, but then we noticed the bulletin flashing
across the screen: civil rights leader Martin Luther King Jr.
had been gunned down in my hometown of Memphis.*

*The TV showed Ralph Abernathy and others huddling
around King, who lay wounded on the terrace of the Lor-
raine Motel. But it was too late. This man who had symbol-
ized the hopes of so many people, this Nobel Peace Prize
winner, had been violently murdered in a nearby, familiar
neighborhood.*

*Things grew quiet around the dinner table—but out-
side in the streets, things were just beginning to heat up.
Violence broke out throughout Memphis. The city was
placed under a dusk-till-dawn curfew. But even that couldn't
stop the looting, rock-throwing and fire-bombing that was
erupting around town.*

*After a few days, most of the violence calmed down.
But in Memphis—as well as hundreds of other cities around
the nation—the tension remained. In 1968, it was going to
be a long, hot summer.*

The death of Martin Luther King in Memphis in 1968
affected people in many different ways. In my case, it forced
me to look at his commitment to his cause and his sacrificial
love for people he didn't even know by name.

King's showdown with destiny in Memphis had really
begun two months earlier with a strike by city sanitation

workers. One day all the city's sanitation workers had been sent home early because of bad weather. But later the black employees discovered that they had been paid for two hours of work while the white employees had received a full day's pay. They went on strike.

After repeated requests, King finally agreed to come to Memphis. He led a protest march which was interrupted by violence. Days later, a 16-year-old black was shot by police. Nearly 300 more people were arrested, and Tennessee's governor ordered 4,000 national guardsmen into the city.

Upset by the violence that engulfed the city, King felt that he had failed. Hoping to demonstrate that nonviolence could still bring about social change, he scheduled another march for April 8. He was preparing for that march when he was shot to death.

Re-evaluating a Fallen Leader

Before King's death, I had seen him as a loud-mouthed, trouble-making opportunist who travelled the country taking advantage of tense racial situations. But as I carefully examined King's life and message, I changed my opinion and came to regard him as a hero—largely because of my growing awareness of how King had bravely sought to do God's will in the face of certain death.

These words, from a King speech shortly before he was shot, stuck in my heart like bullets:

> We've got some difficult days ahead. But it really doesn't matter with me now. Because I've been to the mountain top. I won't mind. Like anybody, I would like to live a long life. Longevity has its place. But I'm not concerned about that now. I just want to do God's will.
> And He's allowed me to go up to the mountain. And I've looked over and I've seen the Promised Land. I may not get there with you, but I want you to know tonight that we as a people will get to the Promised Land.
> So, I'm happy tonight. I'm not worried about anything. I'm

not fearing any man. Mine eyes have seen the glory of
the coming of the Lord.

King's passionate words are powerful even now, and
they have the sound that comes from one who has been in
the presence of Almighty God, and who has been permitted
to look into God's book of things to come and see his own
death. These are the words of a liberator who, like Moses,
valued his life less than he valued the freedom of his people.
And like Moses, King was permitted to view the promised
land, yet was not permitted to enter it himself.

What makes someone a liberator? And why would
anybody in his right mind make the kind of sacrifice King
made? Why would a man give his life to lead his people to
the promised land that he himself would never see?

There's only one explanation. It wasn't bravery. It
wasn't cocky confidence. I believe that, after going to the
mountaintop, King returned to the battlefield because of one
thing: sacrificial love.

Substitutes for Love

What amazes me about King's life and his sacrificial
love is that I seldom have that kind of love myself. It's too
easy to get wrapped up in self and forget that love is my
primary goal.

Jesus tells us that all God's laws and commandments
can be summed up by two things—and both of them are
love: that we love God with all our hearts, and that we love
our neighbor as ourself (Matthew 22:37-40). And Paul tells
us that without love, all our great works and deeds are
worthless (1 Corinthians 13).

During my years of growth and struggle as a Christian
and teacher, I've often lost track of how important love is.
Instead, I've relied on (and told others to rely on) a series of
manmade, religious-sounding substitutes.

As a young Christian, my first substitute for love was
witnessing. No matter what kind of situation I was in or

what the people I was around needed, I felt witnessing was the perfect solution. Please understand: There's nothing wrong with sharing your faith. Eddie and I do it every night in concert because we're committed to giving kids the chance to come to a saving knowledge of Christ. And I still find that telling others about God does *me* a world of good. Yet witnessing alone is no substitute for love.

My second substitute for love was Bible study. As I saw it, the problem with all of humanity was simple: *spiritual ignorance.* I went to Bible college and recommended that every Christian do the same. I filled my head with knowledge. Bible facts literally oozed from my mind.

But it didn't take long to realize how dry my soul could get while absorbing only facts. I began to understand the words of Solomon: "Be warned, my son . . . . Of making many books there is no end, and much study wearies the body" (Ecclesiastes 12:12).

After trying and dismissing these two substitutes, I came up with others: prayer, fasting, fellowship, and more. Each one of these things is essential to the Christian life. Each has its merits. But each left me hungry for the most important thing—love.

Real Love

Thank God I gave up on formulas and began to look to Christ and trust in the simplicity of his love. It sounds simple, but it's profound: the truth that lies within the heart of our faith is this: "God is love."

Love is the reason I am a Christian in the first place.

Love is the reason all of mankind is not hurled headlong into hell.

Love is the reason Christ came to die for fools such as you and me: "For God so loved the world that he gave his one and only Son" (John 3:16). The Bible explains this love to us:

This is how we know what love is; Jesus Christ laid down his life for us. And we ought to lay down our lives for our brothers. If anyone has material possessions and sees his brother in need but has no pity on him, how can the love of God be in him? Dear children, let us not love with words or tongue but with actions and in truth. (I John 3:16)

God showed his love for us by giving. That's how we show our love as well. I'm not talking about the kind of love that the world knows. When people are more interested in taking than in giving, that's lust, not love. Lust is selfish, while true love is selfless.

Watch out when you hear someone say, "I love you, but I can't make any commitments." There is no love without commitments. Love without sacrifice is hollow. Martin Luther King didn't tell the sanitation workers in Memphis, "I care for the people in Memphis, but I can't get involved." Instead, he committed himself to action—even though his actions led to his death.

God didn't tell the human race, "I love you people, but I can't make any commitments." Instead, he backed up his words with actions. It cost Christ his life to prove his love. Real love never does comes cheap.

God wants us to overcome our fears and selfishness and learn to give ourselves away. To do so we need to put Christ before our own desires. That's the most difficult part of sacrificial love.

Sacrificial Love Means Hard Decisions

I don't want to compare myself to Martin Luther King, Moses, or Jesus. It's easier to sing and play music than to risk my life fighting for people's civil rights. But I have asked God to give me sacrificial love—and one of the acts prompted by that love was my decision to play Christian music.

I can already hear some of our critics laughing out loud, saying, "Listen to this guy. He's living a comfortable life. What does he know about making sacrifices?"

And the critics are right, at least partially. Eddie and I

do have comfortable lives—now. But it wasn't always so.

In 1978, when I finally made up my mind to obey God's leading and pursue a full-time music ministry, I sacrificed many things, including a comfortable, well-paying job with Youth for Christ. Believe me, it was scary quitting my job and stepping out on faith. The first five years Eddie and I were out with the band, we were eligible for food stamps. Take my word for it—those were not comfortable years!

I was also sacrificing some peace of mind, since I knew that we would be heading for controversy. I knew that many Christian brothers and sisters didn't understand or agree with what Eddie and I were doing in our music ministry.

I was also committing my wife and children to sacrifice with me! My decision to play Christian music, rather than pursue a business career or a more lucrative secular music career, took food off the family table and kept clothes out of the closet.

My sacrifice also affected my parents. Their dream was that I would become an architect or a lawyer. I wished then that I could have told my folks something that sounded more impressive than, "God has called me into a ministry using 'Jesus Rock.'"

My parents had to make a sacrifice, too. They were called upon by God to give up their desire to see me in a successful business career or with a prestigious education. It was hard to ask them to let go of those dreams. But they gave them up because of their commitment to me and Christ.

These complications made it more difficult for me to have sacrificial love and obey Christ. But as I made these decisions I thought of Jesus' words:

> Anyone who loves his father or mother more than me is not worthy of me; anyone who loves his son or daughter more than me is not worthy of me; and anyone who does not take his cross and follow me is not worthy of me. Whoever finds his life will lose it, and whoever loses his life for my

sake will find it. (Matthew 10:37-39)

When I think about it, I realize that my sacrifices haven't been that tough. My decision to follow Christ hasn't cost me my life, as it did Martin Luther King. Sure, my decision to follow Christ and pursue the ministry of De-Garmo and Key was tough for my parents. Their dream of seeing me become an architect went up in smoke. They saw their son leaving a more traditional and stable type of ministry in Youth for Christ to pursue a music ministry in a radical and unsettled field.

But when Jesus sacrificed his life, he left behind several brothers and his mother with no husband to take care of the family.

Fortunately, God doesn't want us all to go out and risk our lives. But he does want us to be ready to sacrifice ourselves and our pleasures for the good of other people.

Practicing sacrificial love can be costly for you, your family, and your relationships. But there's no way to hide from love if you're serious about serving God.

That's because practicing sacrificial love is necessary for inward peace. Plus, it's the beginning stage of any effective ministry or true love for others. On the other hand, withholding yourself from God will only cause discontentment with yourself and ineffectiveness in your ministry. Learn to give yourself away—and God will open a floodgate of happiness and productivity in your life.

It truly is "more blessed to give than to receive" (Acts 20:35). And I'm not talking about merely giving away your money and possessions. I'm talking about giving away yourself.

Are You Ready to Be a Rebel?

If you ask God to give you a desire for sacrificial love, get ready for some excitement—and maybe even danger!

Look at Martin Luther King. Sacrificial love gave him the power to attack an age-old, "God-ordained" tradition of white superiority. People who love enough to tackle such obstacles often become the object of hatred and violence. Sure enough, King was seen as a rebel, and he was treated in the same manner as other rebels—the same way Pharoah dealt with Moses, the same way Israel dealt with the prophets, and the same way the Pharisees dealt with Jesus. They exterminated him.

Jesus was a rebel, too. He rebelled against the tyrannical chains of religious tradition. While the Pharisees forbade mingling with sinners, Jesus spent much of his time with the "dregs" of society—the tax collectors, prostitutes and other sinners. That's one reason the Sanhedrin (a ruling council of the Jews) grew so irritated with Christ. Their authority depended on the religious traditions Christ sought to destroy.

The Bible paints the picture for us:

> While Jesus was having dinner at Matthew's house, many tax collectors and "sinners" came and ate with him and his disciples. When the Pharisees saw this, they asked his disciples, "Why does your teacher eat with tax collectors and sinners?"
> On hearing this, Jesus said, "It is not the healthy who need a doctor, but the sick. But go and learn what this means: 'I desire mercy, not sacrifice.'" (Matthew 9:10-13)

Finally, Jesus' rebellious ways got Him in trouble. In Matthew 12, he disagreed with the Pharisees about what could be done on the Sabbath. That was the straw that broke the camel's back; after that, the Pharisees plotted to kill Jesus.

God Is Calling You to Be a Liberator

A young boy in a Sunday school class was asked what he had learned from the story of Moses and the burning bush. He replied, "I've learned that if I see a burning bush, I'm going to keep on walking!"

Most of us are like that boy—we're happy to let a

Martin Luther King or a Mother Theresa do the liberating while we mind our own business. Why is that? Is it that we think sacrifice is just for famous Christians and not for us? Is it that most of us haven't been to the mountaintop long enough to catch a vision of sacrificial love?

God wants us all to be liberators. It doesn't take great courage or confidence (Moses didn't have either). All we need is sacrificial love. Courage comes as an outgrowth of love.

Ask God to give you that love, and he may surprise you. Maybe God will open the eyes of your heart to a people in bondage, and you will not be able to rest until you have secured their freedom.

If God gives you that liberating love, thank him. Then ask him to help you—because if you have been enlisted in a divine mission, that mission will cost you. That's why most of us prefer to avoid the struggle and sacrifice by simply looking the other way.

My Point of Decision

Sometimes sacrificial love comes in big ways. Or, it can come in simple ways that we don't expect.

Several years ago, I was faced with a series of difficult decisions. One path seemed safe; the other seemed treacherous. I wanted to take the safe road—even though I knew that the treacherous road was the right one.

Then one night I had a dream. In my dream, I was walking with two friends on our way to a praise service at my church. We were late, so we took a short cut through a dark alleyway. As we walked down the alley, we were startled by the screams of a young man being dragged down the alleyway by two policemen, who cursed and beat him.

They dragged him into a rundown mobile home. We could hear the man's screams, and I was sure we could see the walls of the mobile home vibrating with the impact of their blows.

One of my friends said, "Come on. We've got to rescue

that guy." He ran to the mobile home and began pounding on the door.

My other friend shook his head. "No way," he said. "We gotta get out of here. We're gonna be late for church, and anyway we don't know what this guy has done."

The friend who was beating on the mobile home said, "It doesn't *matter* what he's done. What the police are doing isn't right, and we've got to stop it!"

The other friend responded, "If we do, we'll get beaten up and thrown in jail ourselves. And who do you think people will believe—us or the cops?"

I stood between them, desperately wanting to agree with the one who wanted to continue on to church. But my heart told me that it was my responsibility to stay and do my best to help the man who was being beaten.

I headed toward the mobile home to help, thinking, *How can I explain to my parents and friends why I've been thrown into jail?*

Then I woke up.

I crawled out of bed, got down on my knees, and asked the Lord to give me the love that overcomes the fear of personal injury or the fear of getting a bad reputation. And that is still my prayer, every day.

Now It's Up to You

Are you wondering what all of this has to do with Christian music? Isn't this book supposed to be about Christian music, or something like that? Yes and no. Yes, this book is about music—and about something more important, called ministry.

The music ministry God has called Eddie and me to often runs against tradition. And it hurts us when, because of that, we hear someone say on national television that what we're doing is of the devil.

So far we haven't suffered unto death on a cross, but for a while several years ago we did let criticism bully us into forsaking our calling. We had heard all of the criticism and derision and seen all of the angry, pointed fingers we could stand. We gave up in frustration and discouragement and laid down our music.

We both got jobs, and everything seemed to be going along fine—at least externally. But we weren't at peace with ourselves or with God.

Then a friend named David came to see me. He began talking about the time Christ came to his disciples walking on the water (Matthew 14:22-33). All of the disciples stayed in the boat except for Peter.

"Most people think the point of the story is that Peter didn't have enough faith to walk on the water with Christ—that he failed, and Christ had to reach out his hand and save him." He shook his head. "They're missing it. The point of the story is that Peter was the only one with enough faith to join Jesus in the midst of the storm, while the others were enjoying their safe, dry seats in the boat."

Then David leaned forward and looked right into my eyes. "Dana," he said, "you're one of those disciples still enjoying a safe, secure seat in the boat while Jesus is calling you out into the storm."

This doesn't happen to me very often, but as soon as David said that, I recognized the voice of my Savior. I realized at that moment what I've seen proven many times since—that it's far better to be in the storm where Jesus is than in a dry, safe boat alone.

What is God calling you to do right now? Has he given you love for someone in trouble? Has he put it on your heart to reach out to others in sacrificial, liberating love? Maybe God has shown you people around you who are hurting and lonely and who need you to show them God's love. Maybe God wants you to begin to show some leadership for Christ at school or church, to step out of your comfort zone and to take some risks. Maybe God wants you to give up everything and join a missionary effort—either far away or right in your town or neighborhood.

I don't know what God has called you to do. Only God knows that. But the first step in learning what that call is is turning your life over to him. It is impossible for you to be a channel for Christ's sacrificial love if you have never entered into a personal relationship with him.

Have you given your life to Christ? If not, say this prayer to God. It's very similar to the prayer I spoke in the closet at high school when Christ came into my life:

> Dear Jesus, I am sorry for my sins. Please come into my life and make my heart clean. Thank you for dying on the cross for me.

Or maybe you're already a Christian, but you're confused about the direction of your life and how you are to serve Christ. Success in serving Jesus always begins on your knees. Take a moment and whisper this prayer to God:

> Dear Jesus, thank you for dying for me, and please give me the power to live for you. Lord, please use me anywhere and in any way you desire as I offer to you everything I am and everything I hope to become.

God bless you as you seek to be a channel of God's liberating love.

The DeGarmo & Key Band on stage performing the Tennessee Performing Arts Center in Nashville, TN

Epilogue

Questions and Answers

Hasn't Christian rock become a big money-making industry more than a Christ-serving ministry, and don't Christian rockers bow down to the bottom line?

Your question, which is really quite a few questions, is a good one. And we hear parts of this question in various ways from many people.

First, let me say that for DeGarmo & Key, our goal is serving Christ. Period. Everything else is external. Yes, we sell records and concert tickets, but to us that's no different from a Christian author selling books or a Christian speaker selling films.

A lot has changed in Christian music in the ten years since Eddie and I recorded our first record. An industry of record companies, managers, publicists, magazines, and concert promoters has grown up around Christian rock—basically, because of the law of supply and demand. Surveys say that 90% of Americans believe in God. That means around 200 million Americans are potentially interested in listening to music about God.

We work with some of the "industry" people—after all, if we had to do all the administrative tasks ourselves we'd never have time to sleep, let alone make music. Besides, those people book concerts and manufacture records better than Eddie and I ever could. We make music, and these professionals help us get the music out to people who want it. We work hard to do a professional job and use the resources that are available. I think that's wise, not sinful—especially since we're very careful who we work with.

DeGarmo & Key is not selling the gospel. That is free. But Christian music provides a very important alternative to secular entertainment. The gospel must always be free; entertainment is not.

Not long ago, a Christian brother asked me to come to his church and "share." I told him, "Sure. I'll be glad to." Then he asked, "Will you be needing any help with your equipment?"

I said, "No, friend, there won't be any equipment. I'll only be bringing my Bible." So he made it clear that what he wanted was for me to come and perform, not to come and preach. I assured him that I'd be glad to preach the gospel anytime for free. But giving a free concert is a different matter.

Christians who can afford to pay shouldn't look for handouts in the name of Jesus. Paul received money in exchange for the time and talent it took him to make tents; no doubt Jesus did the same in exchange for his carpentry work. Likewise, Christian musicians should be paid in return for the time and talent required to provide us with good Christian entertainment.

A pastor I know recently told me that he had gone to a Christian businessman and asked to purchase his services, requesting "a good Christian price."

The businessman promptly replied, "Brother, a good Christian price is the price the service or product is worth plus a nice profit for me and my family." I say amen to that.

Hasn't Christian music become a training ground for groups desiring to go "make it" in secular music? Aren't many "Christian" artists merely using the churches as guinea pigs?

Eddie's and my story isn't that unusual in Christian music: We left a promising secular group because we wanted to make music that reflected our faith in Christ.

Maybe ten years ago you could say that Christian music was a place for not-ready-for-prime-time musicians to learn their skills. But now, some of the most talented musicians in the world are recording Christian music: Amy Grant, Russ Taff, Petra, Mylon, and others. The music is better, the albums are better produced, and the concerts are becoming much more professional. Today some nonbelievers may reject Christian music because of its content, but few will reject it because of its quality.

While gospel music may have been a training ground in

the old days, now you have to be very talented to get a toehold in the Christian music world.

Isn't it wrong to place God's timeless message in the "contemporary" package of rock music?

God's message is timeless and unchanging—but the methods of communicating it must be adapted to the ever-changing needs of the particular audience we're trying to reach. I discuss this principal in some detail in chapter 10, "Music and Culture."

Obvious problems can result when two different audiences or cultures dwell side by side. In those cases, the preacher is sometimes left with no choice other than to choose his target audience and adopt appropriate, effective methods of reaching them with the gospel—while getting ready to take the heat from the other, alienated audience that is offended at what he is doing.

Isn't Christian rock filled with shallow messages and weak theology?

Sure, some Christian rock is lightweight. But much of it is solid, sturdy and good. Some of the songs Eddie and I have written have been sung by folks like Sandi Patti and Bill Gaither. And some of our songs appear in hymnals and songbooks.

The lyrics of Christian songs are getting better. It was this improved lyrical quality that helped change the position of former Christian rock hater, Bob Larson. Here's what he said in his book, *Rock:*

> Their local Christian bookstore had stacks of albums by contemporary artists whose music and mode of expression reflect the thinking of young minds. The moods and feelings of adolescent longings are explored with lyrics that are often perceptive and challenging . . . I am more than happy to acknowledge the increasing quality and depth of contemporary Christian musical expression.

So if you're disappointed by the quality of Christian lyrics, hang in there—they're getting better.

Aren't Christian rock concerts just a show and nothing more?

Concerts are often called "shows" by people who attend them, and in many cases they are high-quality, skillfully put together shows. That's why you are asked to pay to get in, just as you would if you were going to see a good movie or play in a theatre.

But behind all the sound, light and glitz, something really significant and positive is happening.

Christian rock concerts provide high-quality Christian entertainment with good spiritual content in a positive moral atmosphere for young people. Kids need this Christian entertainment alternative. And if you don't believe that, check out a secular concert or record and see for yourself.

Christian shows are entertaining, but that's not their main purpose. God has given many contemporary Christian artists special talents and ministry gifts. And it's because of God's blessing that thousands are being won to Christ and challenged to live holy lives each year through these very concerts. In the DeGarmo and Key ministry, we saw more than 5,000 decisions for Christ in one year alone.

I've never met a contemporary Christian artist who didn't make free tickets available to those people who truly needed them. Furthermore, many Christian artists perform benefits for a variety of deserving causes and Christian organizations.

Is it all right to listen to secular music?

Eddie and I hear this question fairly often—maybe because many people misunderstand the distinction between *sacred* and *secular*.

We Christians have failed to see that the *whole earth is the Lord's* — along with everything in it. So we fall into the trap of compartmentalizing the world into *sacred* and *secular.* We think: Going to church is spiritual, but going to work is secular. In God's eyes, going to work is just as much a spiritual duty as going to church.

This compartmentalizing of our lives is artificial and false. All truth is God's. God's truth is no different from other truths, such as the truth that 2 + 2 = 4. The math statement is not "secular" truth, because all truth—theological or mathematical—is God's.

So: Music that reflects God's nature through creativity and beauty is *good* music, whether it is about justification by faith or about the love between a man and a woman.

Here are my recommendations about what music to listen to:

- listen to music of virtue and positive moral value
- listen to music that is performed with skill
- listen to music that helps you love God more, whether or not it is full of Christian lingo.

Those are my recommendations; and now, here's a caution for young Christians coming out of a lifestyle in which rock music was an idol, or who associate rock music with your past sinful lifestyle. It's best not to wallow in the mire of the dark past, but rather to seek God's light. That may mean that, for you, it's better not to listen to any music and to concentrate instead on God and his word. Only you can tell what music is doing to you. Ask God to help you see and to help you make good choices.

The rest of us should follow Pauls'advice about weaker believers in Romans 14. Paul said that nothing of itself was unclean, unless you think it is. If rock music is unclean to you, don't listen to it. And to help you I will not play rock music when you visit my house or ride in my car. I won't force you to eat meat offered to idols or listen to DeGarmo & Key.

What about the origin of rock & roll music? Wasn't it born of sin and the world?

No. In fact, most musicologists agree that rock music was born in American negro churches.

Not too long ago, Eddie and I did a radio interview with a Memphis black celebrity named Honeymoon Garner. When I explained to Mr. Garner that we played contemporary Christian music, he laughed and said, "There's nothing new about that music. We've been doing it in my church for thirty-five years."

Early on, some black singers like Little Richard secularized the music of the church, and replaced "Jesus" with "baby." Then white performers like Elvis and the Beatles followed in these black singers' steps.

But let's forget about history for a minute, and assume that what the critics say is true: that rock & roll did have an illegitimate birth in sin. Does that mean it could never be used by God? Of course not! Ever since the fall of mankind in the book of Genesis we've all been born in sin. Ephesians 2 tells us that we were even enemies of God. Yet we have been redeemed. And even though we are still not without sin, God uses us.

Satan is not the creator of anything, including music. Satan can only pervert that which God originally made for himself, and he has certainly done that with rock music. But the true Creator has the power to redeem and restore that which has fallen into enemy hands and use it for his glory.

Rock is not good or evil. It is a vehicle that can be used for either good or bad purposes. With God's help, we're using it for good.

My parents hate rock music, even with Christian lyrics. Why?

There are two basic reasons parents might dislike rock music.

The first is the easiest to understand: They don't like the sound. It's different from the music they grew up with, and it sounds strange to their ears. They just don't like it.

Another reason many parents don't like rock is because uninformed friends or authors—or maybe even their pastors—have told them that rock is demonic.

Whatever their reasons for disliking rock, most parents

love their children. And, out of a desire to protect their kids from philosophies that are rebellious and destructive, many parents ban rock music. If that's true in your family, be thankful—if your parents watch what you listen to, they must care for you.

Besides—your parents may be justified in criticizing the music you listen to. They may see a parallel between the music you listen to and a specific problem you are having. You may be blind to it, but your parents may have the wisdom to see what you cannot see.

In Memphis, there is a drug and alcohol rehabilitation center called Lakeside. The staff at Lakeside asks kids, as part of their therapy, to stay away from heavy metal for a year. The doctors at Lakeside see an undeniable link between music, mood, and behavior. And I know that, if *I* were a doctor treating adult alcoholics, I would ask them to avoid country music with its talk about drinking and getting wild.

God wants you to obey and love your parents. You can't control how they react to rock music, but you can control how you react to them. Honor your parents, and God will bless you.

Well, then, how can I get my parents to like Christian rock?

If you want to win your parents over to Christian rock, you need to know that your greatest enemy is your parents' lack of familiarity with it. The more your parents know about Christian rock and the people who make the music, the better. All that some parents ever see of the Christian rock world is the lights, the sound, the glitz, and the glitter. They know little of the lifestyles, ministries, or motivations of the artists.

When I was in high school, my older sister, Jolyn, took me to a Halloween costume party to introduce me to some of her friends. When I was first introduced to a couple of gorillas, a clown, and Darth Vader, among others, I thought her friends were pretty weird. But after they took off their masks I realized that we all had much in common.

By the same token, you can't expect your parents to think Christian rockers are anything but weird until they are shown something beneath the surface.

Here's my suggested game plan for winning your parents to the cause:

1. *Obey your parents without begrudging or complaining (Ephesians 6:1).* It's not only the right thing to do but it will also tend to alleviate their fears that Christian rock music is leading you toward sin and rebellion.

2. *Know your stuff.* Research Christian rock performers and educate yourself about their ministries and hearts by reading and collecting interviews, lyrics, or books written by or about Christian rock artists. Check out *Contemporary Christian Music* magazine and *Campus Life* for starters. And carefully read the lyric sheets in your Christian albums.

3. *Look and pray for opportunities to educate your parents* about the goals and aspirations of contemporary Christian music in an atmosphere of love and understanding. Remember, arguing only gives credibility to the false view that rock music breeds rebellion.

4. *Trust God with all of your life, including your entertainment*— remembering that if your parents object to Christian rock it is probably because they love you, and their love is more important than rock & roll (Romans 8:28—29).

Dana sharing between songs during the filming of "Rock Solid... e Rock-u-mentary ".

Questions and Answers

DeGarmo & Key at a Glance

Recordings:
Recordings by DeGarmo & Key
    1989   The Pledge
    1988—Rock Solid—Absolutely Live
    1987—D&K
    1987—Street Rock
    1986—Street Light
    1985—Commander Sozo and the Charge of the Light Brigade
    1984—Communication
    1983—Mission of Mercy
    1982—No Turning Back-Live
    1980—This Ain't Hollywood
    1979—Straight On
    1978—This Time Thru
Solo Recording by Eddie DeGarmo
    1988—Feels Good to Be Forgiven

Awards:
    1989—Grammy Award nomination for D&K

       —Dove Award nominations for Best Rock Song, Best Rock Album, Long-form Video, and Short-form Video - all for "Rock Solid"
    1988—Dove Award nomination for Group of the Year, and Best Rock Album for "D&K"
    1987—Grammy and Dove Award nominations for "Street Light"
    1986—Grammy and Dove Award nominations and Year's Best Album Award, *Campus Life Magazine,* for "Commander Sozo and The Charge of the Light Brigade"
       —Dove Award of Excellence, Memphis Advertising Federation Pyramid Addy Award and *Contemporary Christian Magazine* Video of the Year Award for "Six Six Six"
    1984—Year's Best Album Award, *Campus Life Magazine,* for "Communication"
    1983—Award of Merit, *Group Magazine* and Best Album of the Year, *Contemporary Christian Magazine,* for "Mission of Mercy"
    1981—Grammy Nomination and Year's Best Album Award, *Campus Life Magazine*, for "This Ain't Hollywood"
    1980—Year's Best Album Award, *Campus Life Magazine,* for "Straight On"
    1979—Year's Best Album Award, *Campus Life Magazine,* for "This Time Thru"

Music Video:

    1988—"Rock Solid: The Rock-U-Mentary" (75-minute live
        and documentary footage)
    1987—"Air Care Video" (documentary footage, including Africa
        footage, plus four music videos).
        Produced with Mission Aviation Fellowship.
    1986—"Visions of the Light Brigade" (five concept
        video clips, including original and edited
        versions of "Six, Six, Six."

Songwriting:

DeGarmo & Key have written or co-written songs for the following
    artists:

Amy Grant	White Heart
Sandi Patti	Mylon and Broken Heart
Gaither Vocal Band	Jessy Dixon
Farrell and Farrell	Steve Camp

Televised Guest Appearances and Video Features:

Dove Awards Telecast	700 CLub
CBS Evening News	Crook & Chase
God & Country Special	MTV
Light Music	Hit Video USA
Night Trax	Showtime-Movie Channel
Real Videos	BBC

Recent Concert Appearances:

PARKS:

Knotts Berry Farm, CA	Kansas City Worlds of Fun
Six Flags—Jackson, NJ	Disneyland, CA
Six Flags—Chicago, IL	Magic Mountain Amusement Park
Six Flags—Santa Clara, CA	Dollywood, TN
Six Flags—Arlington, TX	Opryland, TN
King's Dominion, VA	

FESTIVALS/CONVENTIONS:

Charleston Regatta	Jesus '89, Florida Festival
Creation Festival '89	Jesus Northwest '89
Atlanta Fest	Detroits Main Event
Fishnet '89	Youth Specialties Conv. '89
Ichthus '89	Dove Awards '89
Encounter '89	Cornerstone Festival

Books:

This is it, so far!

Management: Brock & Associates, 1105 16th Ave. So.,Suite C
Nashville, TN 37212 (615) 327-1880